WHAT'S YOUR LEADERSHIP STORY?

WHAT'S YOUR LEADERSHIP STORY?

A School Leader's Guide to Aligning
How You Lead with Who You Are

GRETCHEN OLTMAN
VICKI BAUTISTA

Alexandria, Virginia USA

1703 N. Beauregard St. • Alexandria, VA 22311-1714 USA
Phone: 800-933-2723 or 703-578-9600 • Fax: 703-575-5400
Website: www.ascd.org • Email: member@ascd.org
Author guidelines: www.ascd.org/write

Ranjit Sidhu, *CEO & Executive Director*; Penny Reinart, *Chief Impact Officer*; Genny Ostertag, *Senior Director, Acquisitions and Editing*; Susan Hills, *Senior Acquisitions Editor*; Julie Houtz, *Director, Book Editing*; Jamie Greene, *Editor*; Thomas Lytle, *Creative Director*; Donald Ely, *Art Director*; Masie Chong, *Graphic Designer*; Kelly Marshall, *Production Manager*; Circle Graphics, *Typesetter*; Shajuan Martin, *E-Publishing Specialist*; Christopher Logan, *Senior Production Specialist*

PAPERBACK ISBN: 978-1-4166-3039-5   ASCD product #121020   n8/21
PDF E-BOOK ISBN: 978-1-4166-3040-1; see Books in Print for other formats.
Quantity discounts are available: email programteam@ascd.org or call 800-933-2723, ext. 5773, or 703-575-5773. For desk copies, go to www.ascd.org/deskcopy.

Library of Congress Cataloging-in-Publication Data

Names: Oltman, Gretchen A. author. | Bautista, Vicki, author.
Title: What's your leadership story? : a school leader's guide to aligning how you lead with who you are / Gretchen Oltman & Vicki Bautista.
Description: Alexandria, VA : ASCD, 2021. | Includes bibliographical references and index.
Identifiers: LCCN 2021019032 (print) | LCCN 2021019033 (ebook) | ISBN 9781416630395 (paperback) | ISBN 9781416630401 (pdf)
Subjects: LCSH: Educational leadership. | School management and organization. | Conduct of life.
Classification: LCC LB2806 .O48 2021 (print) | LCC LB2806 (ebook) | DDC 371.2—dc23
LC record available at https://lccn.loc.gov/2021019032
LC ebook record available at https://lccn.loc.gov/2021019033

30 29 28 27 26 25 24 23 22 21   1 2 3 4 5 6 7 8 9 10 11 12

WHAT'S YOUR LEADERSHIP STORY?

A Letter to the Reader

Dear Reader,

    As we wrote this book, we envisioned the school leader who sees the cover of the book and connects with the idea of a leadership "story." There's something about you—someone working, teaching, and leading in today's school—that longs to be better understood, but the words are hard to find. You became a school leader through your own unique path and possess a set of talents that sets you apart from others. You most likely work tirelessly to serve students, teachers, and the school community. But there's something about the public, yet distant, connection to your job—your rank or position—that causes others to make inaccurate or unfair assumptions about you.

    This is natural. After all, schools have had the same leadership structures for decades. Even as we've expanded and dispersed leadership responsibilities to other roles, such as teacher leaders, assistant principals, mentors, instructional coaches, and department chairs, we remain working in a field where serving in a leadership role causes others to presume how we are supposed to lead.

Even though we naturally want to be understood by those we work with and invest our time in, the sometimes directionless path we feel often consumes our work. Long days, heavy workloads, and challenging responsibilities can leave us functioning in a reactionary mode. We do our best to stay centered and maintain a balance of a well-lived life, but we sometimes fail because the demands of the job are more pressing than our personal well-being. We know, deep down, that leadership must be strategic. We know we must be purposeful about how we lead. We know our school community deserves a leader who has a solid foundation in ethical and moral principles. Nevertheless, there's just not enough time in the day to reflect and renew these commitments.

You've opened this book at precisely the right time. Not only will we embark on a process to help others understand your leadership story, but we will lead you through a process to purposefully engage in meaningful self-reflection to better design your leadership philosophy. Additionally, the challenges that have faced school leaders, even in the brief time we spent writing this book, have been monumental. We would be remiss not to recognize that during our writing and revising process, a worldwide pandemic shuttered the doors of most schools, and school leaders were faced with decisions unlike any they faced before. The public criticism, debate, and targeted attacks on the decisions of school leaders were unprecedented—and for the most part, unwarranted. As we watched this take place, we became even further convinced that school leaders operating with a foundational personal leadership philosophy would have found solace in knowing and defending why and how their decisions to protect students and staff, often by closing schools and reinventing education, were grounded in their core values and a growth-focused mindset. If nothing else, the personal leadership philosophy—your leadership story—serves as a personalized map when there is no clear direction in which to head.

Philosophy is a heavy word. It reminds us of the great thinkers of centuries gone by: Socrates, Plato, Aristotle, Amo, and Kant. It is the pursuit of wisdom and an articulation of our most basic beliefs, concepts, and attitudes. Today, few of us consider ourselves philosophers, yet this desire that you have to be better understood, to make decisions from a grounded place, and to enjoy meaningful relationships is just that.

The personal leadership philosophy process is an exploration of these basic fundamentals that make you who you are today. In our journey to craft a personal leadership philosophy together, here in these pages, we think you will discover a sense of purpose, renewal, and inspiration that may have slipped away amid the chaos of life.

With this mindset, we welcome you to this expedition. In this trek, we hope you will find encouragement, advice, and motivation for your leadership. We already know your story is unique, and we look forward to hearing from you as you put your personal leadership philosophy into practice.

Best Regards,
Gretchen and Vicki

How Can I Be More Than My Title?

Jake was transitioning from his job as a 6th grade history teacher to becoming the school's new assistant principal. In the classroom, Jake had an obvious rapport with the students—so much so that they voted him "Most Popular Teacher" two years in a row. His laidback teaching style was engaging and non-threatening, and he had a way of connecting with students that helped even the most reluctant learner want to know more about history.

As Jake began his new job, he was asked to deal with a former student of his who had just gotten kicked out of music class for disrupting the choir rehearsal. Jake sat down with the student, began to talk through why the student was behaving as he was, and eventually told the student that he would have to serve a detention for his class disruption.

The student immediately grew angry. "You used to be so cool," he said, "but now you're just one of them!" Suddenly, Jake realized that he was unprepared to accept what people thought of him in his new role as an administrator. What had happened to him?

Has anyone ever expected you to behave or act a certain way simply *because* you are a school leader? Consider our colleague, Andrea, an assistant superintendent who told us she is forced to shop in a certain part of town because community members are constantly watching her at the grocery store just to see how much she spends. Another school leader joked about not being able to exceed the speed limit because a ticket would be a black mark on her reputation. One teacher leader shared with us the struggles of meeting with her own children's teachers, noting that she felt they were reluctant to be forthright with her because of her position. An instructional coach told us about a time she shared a vacation photo on her personal social media page and faced critical comments from parents who questioned why she was not at work or how she could afford to take a vacation with her public school paycheck. Yet another school leader reported that he noticed a change in demeanor when he attended a school parents' meeting for one of his own children, with parents seated around him quickly ending conversations.

Many people make wrongful assumptions about school leaders or have unrealistic expectations for them because of the roles they fill at school. Imagine taking over for the retiring school principal only to be told you have to do things the exact same way she did. Or imagine being told by a team of teachers you are failing at your job because you choose to do things differently or challenge the existing norms in a building. We often teach our students to be resilient in the face of others' opinions, but it can be hard to take this advice when you are in a school leadership position. People will always have an opinion about how well you do your job and whether you are qualified to make the decisions you do. This book is designed to help you solidify your strengths as a leader, your qualities as a human, and your path as an educator. Although others may question or criticize you, one of the best professional tools you can create is a personal leadership philosophy (PLP) that clearly lays out who you are and what you hope to accomplish professionally.

You are so much more than your title—a friend, relative, leader, companion, colleague. Your title just explains the role you play professionally within a school setting. In a sense, you hold two identities: one based on your own lived experiences, mindset, core values, and personal leadership style, and another based on your title and perceived mainly by others. If these two identities conflict in some way, there can be problems. However, if you can authentically tell your story so your school community can know you, what you value, and why you make decisions the way you do, then you will build a stronger connection with those you lead and work beside.

Consider This

 Think about your two identities—who you are in your everyday personal life and who you appear or are assumed to be in your role as a professional. Create a list of words that describe you in each role (thinking particularly about how others would describe you). Write those words here:

Personal Identity

_____

_____

_____

_____

_____

Professional Identity

_____

_____

_____

_____

_____

Now reflect on why some people might perceive you differently than you perceive yourself. Maybe your students think you are a strict rule-enforcer, but you know you are really a student-safety advocate. Or perhaps your colleagues perceive you as easygoing when in reality you are attempting to allow for shared decision making.

Find these "collisions of identity" and write about one here. Why do you think these different perceptions exist? How do you know the "collision of identity" is present? Where and when have you felt it? How does it make you feel in the midst of realizing someone is relating to you in your professional role rather than for who you really are?

_____

_____

_____

_____

_____

Being a leader can cause you to act differently in your professional role than you might in your personal life, and that makes complete sense. This can be especially noticeable when you serve a broad variety of constituencies. During the course of one day, school leaders might interact with students, teachers, parents, community members, fellow school leaders, alumni, and school board members in addition to our own friends and family members. With our students, we may try to come off as light-hearted or approachable. With school board members, we may want to seem decisive and in control. With our own families, we may be quiet and compassionate. Authentic leaders who lead with clarity and purpose find room for all necessary facets of their different identities to coexist.

Consider This

 Esther has been a high school principal for 20 years. Before stepping into this role, she served as an art teacher, leading the district art curriculum adoption process and cofounding the student art show. As a principal, Esther is known for her witty disposition and relentless pursuit of behavior management within classrooms, but few would guess that she has an artistic side; she seems more like a rule-follower than a creative spirit.

Think of some ways Esther can merge her artistic and rule-driven leadership sides. What might she do to bring more of her personal side into her work world?

After some careful reflection, Esther accepted that she did not want to isolate her artistic side from her professional life. Therefore, she began to bring her love of art into the school—first by painting a mural near the school entrance illustrating the school's diversity and inclusive mission, then by commissioning teachers and students to paint other pictures throughout the school, bringing life to the drab hallways. She also made it a priority to advocate for arts funding in her annual budget meetings with the superintendent.

Leading in a school setting does not mean you should lose your individual identity. By working purposefully to share your leadership background, lived experiences, core values, and mindset about education with others, you can create a new expectation of what a school leader should be that reflects how unique and independent you are.

Why We Wrote This Book

Our experiences working with educators and with leaders from multiple disciplines have taught us that even though most educators can articulate a teaching philosophy, the same cannot be said of leaders and a leadership philosophy. Why is this? Many job interviews and applications for teaching positions require applicants to share their personal teaching philosophy, but few of the same requirements apply to those moving into leadership positions. Again, why is this? Why is a philosophy necessary in the classroom but not to lead an institution? What does that say about the value we place on our philosophies or guiding practices in the first place?

Unfortunately, there is little clear guidance as to what makes up a complete leadership philosophy. We have read books, websites, journal articles, magazines, and blogs seeking an easy-to-implement formula for our aspiring leadership students only to come up empty-handed. We immediately understood that this lack of resources directly affects school leaders of all kinds—principals, superintendents, teacher leaders, instructional coaches, curriculum directors, even staff. In our own work, we have observed that most educators don't really have a clear idea as to *why* their leaders lead the way they do or how to articulate an alternative leadership approach.

We hope you approach this book as a workbook, scratching notes into the margins and using it to reflect honestly on leadership. The book walks you through a variety of self-assessments and reflective prompts to help you tell your leadership story. Each self-assessment will provide insight about your leadership attributes to help you build an approachable, concise personal leadership philosophy that you can share with your school community. You will be challenged to engage with trusted colleagues, consider your leadership attributes honestly, and bring your leadership story to life.

Teaching Philosophy vs. Leadership Philosophy

It is important to distinguish between a teaching philosophy and a leadership philosophy. Most teachers enter the classroom with a teaching philosophy of some sort—a set of expectations for how to guide students, aspirations for student learning, and perhaps personal reflections about the meaning of learning. By contrast, a leadership philosophy outlines what followers can expect and identifies a cohesive strategy for leading followers and colleagues. Both philosophies require the educator to be self-aware and reflective and are effective when they accurately represent the educators' true beliefs and abilities.

Consider This

If you have a teaching philosophy available, use it for this exercise. If you don't, think about your initial years as an educator and how you would have answered these questions then.

What beliefs about education does your teaching philosophy reveal?

_____

_____

_____

_____

_____

What does your teaching philosophy say about how you will teach?

_____

_____

_____

_____

_____

What does your teaching philosophy identify as evidence of good teaching?

_____

_____

_____

_____

_____

When did you last revise your teaching philosophy and why?

_____

_____

_____

_____

_____

Who has read your teaching philosophy? Have you received any feedback on it? If so, did it lead you to change your philosophy in any way?

_____

_____

_____

_____

_____

It is fairly common for teachers to develop a teaching philosophy prior to beginning their first job and to share it both with students and the greater school community. However, over time, experience can reshape our philosophies. This evolution reflects both the continually shifting nature of education and our own evolution as educators. What worked yesterday does not always work today; likewise, what works with one group of students may be completely ineffective with another group. Flexibility, adaptability, and a willingness to learn are crucial. The same goes for school leaders. Every year presents new challenges, people, decisions, and disappointments. Leaders must be just as adaptable to change as teachers, and they are just as likely as teachers to see shifts in their philosophy over time.

Building a Personal Leadership Philosophy

Your personal leadership philosophy (PLP) is a reflective explanation of the leadership style, core values, mindset, and real-life experiences that make you the leader you are today. It should be no more than one page long and written in everyday wording free from jargon or insider language, and you should periodically revisit it to see if it needs readjusting to reflect changes to your philosophy.

The process of building a PLP helps you identify your unique characteristics, traits, and attributes. It relies on how you perceive your own life, the things and ideas that you value, and the experiences that formed your thinking. In developing a PLP, you are also creating a map to help others (your followers, most importantly) understand and appreciate how and why you lead the way you do.

Imagine being able to explain your leadership style, your core values, your mindset, and how your experiences shape your thinking in under five minutes. You would immediately telegraph that you embrace who you are and how you lead. To your followers and colleagues, you would appear confident and prepared. In your heart, you'd know you were just being you.

Everyone Is a Leader

Leadership is more than a title, position, or paycheck. Certainly, school leaders will have titles or positions that reflect leadership terminology and roles that require decision making and strategizing, but ineffective leaders with formal titles may not actually be leading at all, and some of our best leaders are not identified as such by their titles.

A walking tour through a typical school shows what we mean. As we enter the office, we greet the school secretary. Her voice welcomes all visitors in person, immediately setting the tone for how they perceive the building; she also closely guards the confidential communications of teachers and students and has a key to every classroom. We then wave to the assistant principal, who is meeting with a student and her parents about her recent lack of attendance. We stop by the principal's office, where we find the principal working on a budget and trying to determine class sizes for the next semester. Out in the hallway, we run into a custodian fixing a locker. Without his work ethic, the safety of students would be compromised. We overhear the choir teacher conducting students through a new song and the Spanish teacher reviewing verbs with his class. We then visit the lunchroom, where the lunch team is conducting a safety audit and revisiting a recent change in nutrition guidelines.

Clearly, not everyone who makes leadership decisions has a title or position that says so. In fact, schools need every single adult within them to make informed, ethical leadership decisions every day, often without the guidance or input of administrators. That is what makes our schools strong and our institutions trustworthy. We develop our staff to know how and why to make decisions in a way that puts student learning first and allows everyone in the building the autonomy to make decisions.

For those of us with formal leadership roles, acknowledging that we don't make every decision in the building can be hard. But let's be real: we don't. And for our leadership to be effective, we have to share our vision, beliefs, and values with everybody else who makes decisions with or without our presence.

Growing into Your Leadership Role

Embracing the idea that every person in your school is a leader is not meant to minimize your position or title. You achieved your leadership role through hard work, dedication, and investing in your education. Certainly, you have the authority to make decisions on behalf of your school, teachers, and parents, and you represent them in a variety of capacities. Your role is integral to the daily functioning of the school or school system.

Moving into a leadership position can be stressful, even for those who've been preparing for it their whole careers. New responsibilities, new constituents, and challenging decisions can quickly cause new leaders to burn out or start doubting themselves. For this reason, one of the most important traits leaders can have is the ability to pause and reflect on their role. Leading should not require you to change who you are or what you fundamentally believe, but it does require you to learn, evolve, and shift your practice as you gain experience.

Accidental Leadership

Many people holding leadership positions in schools and universities never actually aspired to be leaders. Imagine that—your dean, principal, superintendent, or governor may not have even wanted the job in the first place! We call these folks "accidental leaders." Many only ever wanted to be teachers but either were amazing at their jobs or in the right place at the right time and ended up as leaders. One department chair shared with us that she was appointed to the position because she happened to be the only person who answered the phone the day the principal was calling around asking for someone to take the role. You might even be an accidental leader yourself.

Of course, doing a different job well or simply being available are not enough to ensure that someone can flourish as a leader. Teachers who are exceptional in the classroom are not always great administrators, and principals who lead with ease may find struggles as superintendents. A PLP is especially important to accidental leaders because they are often behind with regard to training, mental preparation, and being able to articulate a leadership philosophy. In this book, we offer a step-by-step process that allows educators who had not set out to be leaders to identify and highlight their leadership attributes.

When You Don't Feel Like a Leader

Many school leaders we've worked with, even those who had always wanted to be in leadership positions, have revealed to us that they don't "feel" like leaders. They are plagued by self-doubt, insecurity, and a sense of fragility. For these leaders, too, building a PLP can prove helpful. When you are able to identify your leadership style, core values, mindset, and relevant life experiences, you can more clearly appreciate why you're fit to be a leader.

> **Consider This**
>
>
>
> *When do you make assumptions about others based on their job title? Think about your doctor, attorney, babysitter, mechanic. Do you have some internal assumptions about who this person is and how he or she should behave? Where did you form these assumptions? And how did these assumptions change over time?*

How to Use This Book

This book will guide you through the following eight steps necessary to draft, revise, and reflect upon your PLP:

1. Identifying your leadership style.
2. Defining your core values.
3. Engaging with your mindset.
4. Exploring your real-life experiences.
5. Creating a draft of your leadership philosophy.
6. Reflecting on your leadership philosophy.
7. Revising your leadership philosophy.
8. Sharing your leadership philosophy.

The first four steps in the process require you to recognize some specific traits about yourself and your leadership preferences, style, and dispositions, and the ensuing steps encourage you to put what you know to be true about yourself into words that will shape your philosophy. Along the way, we share examples to help you. Each chapter includes engaging features that ask you to do more than read the book and set it aside, including these:

-   "Consider This" sections, where you will read about school leaders and respond to a series of questions about the issues they face.

- Reflective questions to promote independent thought and discussion.
- Real-life stories from school leaders we've met, read about, or observed in practice.

To get the most out of this book, we suggest that you read each chapter independently and spend time engaging with the scenarios and reflective questions. There are no right or wrong answers—what you are doing here is crafting your leadership story. What you write will look different than what every other reader will write, and that is as it should be. We hope that as you engage in this process, you will start to actively think more about what it means for you to be a leader—as you commute to work, as you walk the hallways, and as you interact with your school community.

Reflection Questions

1. Think of a time when someone treated you based on your title instead of how you really are. How did this make you feel?
2. What assumptions do people make about you as a school leader? How did you learn about these assumptions? How does knowing about these assumptions change your behavior?
3. Do you treat every person in your building as though they are a leader in their own way? How?
4. When can our assumptions about people's formal titles be helpful? Identify a time when assumptions about someone's role proved to be wise.
5. What are some key points in your teaching philosophy? How have your priorities changed over time, and why?
6. What do you wish others understood about you?
7. Reflect on a time when you treated a member of your community as a leader even though they didn't hold a formal leadership role.
8. Did you aspire to be a leader? What do you hope to gain from your leadership role?

2

Effects of the PLP on Today's Leaders

It is important to be aware of the impact a PLP can have on your colleagues, students, and school community. In this chapter, we present some of the ways PLPs have made a difference in real schools across the country.

An Elevator Speech for Educators

One of the strengths of a PLP is its brevity. One principal calls it an "elevator speech for educators," and we agree. Few educators have the time or energy to read lengthy philosophy statements, so we must be able to explain our leadership style, core values, mindset, and relevant real-life experiences succinctly. If people ask why academic achievement is so important to you, relate it to your core values. If they ask what style of leader you are, your PLP can lead to more meaningful conversation. Although we may not find ourselves in many elevators, we do often find ourselves in conversations where time is limited, and a PLP can be very helpful at those times.

Improved Collaboration Among the School Community

School leaders, teachers, and other school personnel can sit around a table and work through the PLP process together, allowing for improved collaboration. One school used a summer retreat to allow each building administrator to write and share a PLP. This process resulted in the creation of a dialogue around what had been merely assumed or left unspoken for many years. The PLP process allowed this team to eliminate assumptions and hear from everyone in their own words. The ensuing school year began with a new shared understanding of leadership talents and abilities.

School leaders can collaborate on PLPs for all staff, not just those with leadership titles or who work directly with students. Larger group explorations that include secretarial staff, custodial workers, and nutrition workers can create a common dialogue around the notion of everyday leadership and shared responsibility for caring for the entire school community.

Improved Academic Achievement

When we first developed the PLP process to help students in graduate classrooms articulate their leadership philosophies, we were encouraged by the idea that leaders who know how and why they lead can actually improve the academic achievement of their students. Though the tie between a PLP and academic achievement has not been confirmed through research, we know there *is* a correlation between school leaders who recognize their talents and improved student achievement. Waters, Marzano, and McNulty (2004), writing about 21 identifying characteristics of school leadership that affect academic achievement, identified the leader's own knowledge base about leadership as the most effective. "It can be said that if you want to change the world," they wrote, "start by looking in the mirror" (p. 51).

Recognized and Appreciated Personal Traits

Sharing a PLP can make colleagues aware of talents and skills they may not otherwise know about one another. For example, one teacher we know had never told her colleagues about her exceptional art skills; when her PLP revealed creativity as one of her core values, the dynamics of her teaching team changed—she took on leadership to design a mural in the school's entrance, she integrated creative options into her student-choice projects, and she began to lead an afterschool faculty art studio. She was recognized for something that she hadn't been recognized for before. In another case, a school principal surprised his staff by sharing in his PLP that he grew up working on a farm. As Mooney and Mausbach (2008) write,

> Principals and central office administrators who want school improvement that lasts must identify their own core values and beliefs. Trust and respect grow in a climate where leaders lead from their own high moral ground and good character. All the school improvement processes in the world cannot cover up for serious character flaws. Ultimately, the level of trust and respect that followers have for their leaders determines their success. Reflecting on the importance of building trust and respect, identifying core values and beliefs, and acting within a framework of honesty and integrity are necessary steps for effective supervision. (p. 127)

The PLP allows you to identify what matters most to you. In doing so, you may reveal to your colleagues some of your lesser-known—yet very valuable—talents.

Reinforced Values in Challenging Circumstances

When the COVID-19 pandemic arrived in 2020, we wondered how the PLP would help school leaders navigate such uniquely challenging times. As it turns out, the PLP survived the pandemic quite well. Identifying their core values, mindset, and styles helped educators articulate how they thought they should handle educating students remotely.

One school leader shared the heavy weight of her commitment as she communicated to the staff, parents, and students at her school about pandemic-related measures. She said she frequently revisited her core value of responsibility as she measured whether her school was adequately meeting the needs of her students. Another school leader delivered meals to students he knew would not be getting enough to eat at home. He shared that he recognized how the little things he did affected the lives of the students who could not be in school—something that was evident in his servant leadership style.

Clearer Pathways to Leadership

In developing the PLP process and in our workshops with academic leaders, we began to see trends in how professionals move into leadership positions. We ran into our fair share of accidental leaders—those who stumbled into unintended or unwanted leadership positions—but we also met with a good number of leaders seeking to advance professionally into bigger and better jobs. As we worked with this latter group on their PLPs, it became obvious that lack of guidance regarding the development of a leadership philosophy represented a gaping hole in professional development. One aspiring high school dean summed his leadership philosophy up in four pages before committing to the PLP process. Another education leader shared how her PLP had become her personal brand—a succinct way to share her story to those who did not know her or have the time to listen to her life story. These examples, as shared by practicing school leaders, indicated that they had no guidance or framework at all when developing a philosophy and were working from scratch. Some were developing marketing statements, some were writing aspirational essays, and others were solely focused on job performance as a measure of success.

Professional goals are purposefully not part of the PLP. Although it is clearly important to identify these, the PLP is not meant to predict the future. One teacher found that removing the goal of becoming a principal from her draft PLP opened the door for her to explore a variety of potential leadership positions.

Relatable and Approachable School Leaders

One of the most enjoyable moments of our PLP workshops comes when we invite participants to share stories about what they learned from the very first jobs they held (sometimes many, many years ago). Often, these represent essential services—cleaning toilets, selling sandwiches, even playing the piano at funerals. Without fail, every participant we have ever met has been able to apply lessons from those first jobs to their current job as a leader. When they make that connection, it is like a lightbulb goes off—at some level, in some way, our leaders are still living the lessons from those first jobs. Often, our workshop conversations help educators open a dialogue with parents and students, and among staff, a "distant principal" might be more relatable after sharing stories from her days as a waitress or retail store employee.

Renewed, Reinvigorated, and Reminded Educators

Perhaps the most important effect of a PLP is the renewal it affords educators. School leaders who work through the process explain that it allows them to reexamine why they are in leadership positions in the first place. Many finally recognize that they never wanted to be leaders and may even reevaluate their career paths. Others become more aware of their strengths and unique talents and how to better use them to serve their schools. One leader we know was driven by her work on the PLP to build stronger relationships with the adults in her building—from the custodians to the most veteran teachers. She said that if she used her ability to connect with her teachers, she knew her teachers would in turn connect in a more meaningful way with students. Further, an instructional coach told us that after she posted her PLP on the door to her office, conversations with parents, teachers, and students ensued that helped renew her enthusiasm for her work.

Conclusion

In the time we've spent with educators working through, revising, and wordsmithing PLPs, we've felt the hunger educators have for direction, self-discovery, and reflection. Working in school leadership can kill you (sometimes literally: we've worked with educators whose stress levels led to premature death), but it does not have to be that way. Today's school leaders can and should have a clear understanding of why they do what they do and how their unique history is an advantage—not a detriment. Rather than trying to fit all leaders into the same mold, why not embrace their individuality? After all, it is what we seek to do with our students—welcome diversity, differences, unique talents, and perspectives. Our students will achieve bigger and better things if our leaders are allowed to do the same.

Reflection Questions

1. Why is it important for a school leader to have contemplated and articulated a personal philosophy?
2. How could your communication strategy change if your philosophy and guiding principles were better known to your school community?
3. In what ways do you wish your school community understood your background?

4. What makes you unique as a school leader? How do you approach things differently than others?

5. What do others often compliment you on with regards to your leadership? What are some frequent points of criticism?

6. What professional aspirations do you have? How realistic are these goals?

7. What role does your leadership play in student achievement?

8. How does your leadership affect teacher well-being?

9. In what ways do you seek out mentorship from other leaders?

10. Who has been the most influential leader to you? Why?

3

What Is My Leadership Style?

Athletic director Matt was first to arrive and last to leave on game days. He carried unused equipment in the back of his truck just in case it was needed, and whenever an athlete forgot a snack for the bus, he was prepared with extras in hand. During the summer, Matt mowed the football field—not because he had to but because he felt like he was the only one who cared enough to do it well, with straight lines and enough water to survive the desert heat.

When Matt interviewed for this job, he was asked to identify his leadership style. "Always ready," he responded. This was true—Matt was always ready for any possible circumstance and was probably more prepared than most other athletic directors on an average day. However, he was also much more than "always ready." He was consistently setting an example to the coaches and athletes he worked with, motivating others to excel, and demonstrating service in action.

A leadership style is sometimes described as a leader's approach to providing direction, implementing plans, and motivating people (Kotter, 2000). Think about your roles throughout the day: you work with teachers, navigate student problems, communicate with parents, and send multiple emails to school community members. Regardless of your formal role as administrator, principal, instructional coach, or teacher, you often find yourself managing multiple roles with different people. With your teaching staff, you might be a mentor. With your colleagues, you might take on the role of motivational coach. With students, you might be an authority figure providing guidance about rules and expectations. Your leadership style is bound to be relatively similar in all of these contexts.

The Three Main Leadership Styles

There are three commonly observed leadership styles, often referred to as *authoritarian, democratic,* and *laissez-faire.* In this book, we will refer to them as *directing, guiding,* and *enabling.* After reading the descriptions of each leadership style in this chapter, answer the relevant "Consider This" questions. At the end of the chapter, you will complete a short self-assessment to help you better identify and articulate which style best fits your work as a school leader today.

Directing Leadership

Directing leaders are those who perceive their employees as needing ongoing direction to complete work-related tasks. These leaders have a lot of control over their employees and motivate them by strictly enforcing rules, regulations, and consequences. When they provide praise and criticism, these are based on their personal standards instead of objective measures (Northouse, 2015).

The directing leadership style is most effective when there is limited room for error or when used with new staff who might initially require close monitoring. This style is effective when helping a new front office secretary learn the duties associated with the position, for example, or when guiding a new administrator through learning policies and protocols.

Directing leaders are sometimes seen in a negative light because of their strict approach. Most employees do not want or need to be told what to do; rather, they prefer to be encouraged or coached. Still, the directing leadership style can sometimes be necessary in schools—such as during the COVID-19 pandemic, when school leaders were charged with making unilateral decisions to protect the health and well-being of students and staff. Because time was of the essence, leaders had to make these kinds of decisions without much input from others.

Consider This

When have you used the directing leadership style?

_____

_____

_____

_____

_____

When might you use the directing leadership style?

_____

_____

_____

_____

_____

Guiding Leadership

The guiding leadership style centers on shared decision-making and problem-solving responsibilities. Leaders who exhibit this style encourage team members to share ideas with them and create their own realistic goals and evaluate their performance regularly. Guiding leaders treat others as fully capable of completing their work, aim to treat everyone fairly, and speak at the same level as those they lead (Northouse, 2015). The guiding style is especially suitable when building a culture of empowerment and engagement within a school building.

Guiding leaders tend to guide others through questions rather than directives. For instance, rather than telling a teacher how a misbehaving student should be disciplined, the guiding leader might ask that teacher for ideas on how best to deal with the student. Alternatively, when a staff member struggles with a difficult parent, a guiding leader might step in as a mediator. The guiding style can be used with students, too, such as by inviting their opinions on school events or school policy changes, ensuring they have a seat at the table when important decisions are made.

Consider This

When have you used the guiding leadership style?

_____

_____

_____

_____

_____

When might you use the guiding leadership style?

_____

_____

_____

_____

_____

Enabling Leadership

At the other end of the spectrum from the directing leadership style lies the enabling leadership style. This approach takes decision-making responsibility off the shoulders of leaders and places it in the hands of staff, teachers, and students. Enabling leaders trust that their employees will get the job done with minimal supervision and give them a wide latitude to carry out their responsibilities. These leaders generally allow their followers to work on their own time (within reason, of course) and to have complete control over their goals (Amanchukwu, Stanley, & Ololube, 2015).

Enabling leaders must ensure that those they entrust with responsibility are motivated self-starters who know how to complete the task at hand and who are willing to reach out to the leader when they need guidance and feedback. This type of leadership style allows for a great deal of autonomy among staff, which most educators welcome—but which also means that reluctant decision makers will need to find ways to solve problems and resolve conflicts without involving the leader.

Consider This

When have you used the enabling leadership style?

_____

_____

_____

_____

_____

When might you use the enabling leadership style?

_____

_____

_____

_____

_____

Additional Leadership Styles

Although most leadership styles fall into one of these three categories, leaders working in education may also exhibit characteristics of transformational, transactional, instructional, or servant leadership styles.

Transformational Leadership

Transformational leaders are willing to adapt as students, teachers, and the greater educational context change over time. These leaders tend to be willing to take risks and innovate (Bass & Avolio, 1994). They are open to letting followers be creative and try out new ideas. As Smith (2016) notes, "Transformational leaders are not intimidated by change and lead in a manner that supports organizational change and supports those who are willing to try new things" (p. 67). Teachers and students led by transformational leaders are accustomed to a growth mindset that accepts failure as a part of the process of innovation.

Many school leaders aspire to be transformational because to do otherwise in a world where new ideas, teaching methods, learning technology, and student resources are constantly evolving can mean being left behind and out of touch.

Transactional Leadership

The transactional leader sees education as an exchange of goods or services. Consider the superintendent who negotiates extra materials with a new curriculum package purchase, for example, or who approves higher salaries for teachers on the condition that they complete additional evaluations. This kind of leader is focused on the process of setting expectations and rewarding workers for meeting them (St. Thomas University, 2018) and is often a great negotiator who builds support through strategic planning.

Instructional Leadership

Put simply, instructional leaders focus on student learning more than anything else. They always consider how student learning will be affected when making decisions, and they never allow other matters to interfere with their overall focus of teaching and learning. These kinds of leaders are especially necessary in schools as standards and formal assessments become more and more ingrained. Like transformational leaders, instructional leaders are often willing to challenge norms and promote innovation and creativity.

Servant Leadership

"A servant-leader focuses primarily on the growth and well-being of people and the communities to which they belong" (Robert K. Greenleaf Center for Servant Leadership, 2016). Servant leaders always put service to others first; they also tend to share power and seek ways to help coworkers solve challenges. Due perhaps to the caretaking mentality of so many educators, these kinds of leaders are plentiful in schools. We know administrators who buy school supplies out of their own pockets, keep a supply of breakfast bars on hand for students who show up to school late and hungry, and can be found cleaning up spilled milk in the cafeteria at lunch time.

Shifts in Leadership Styles

Leaders can embody aspects of different styles depending on the context and transition from one style to another quickly and without much warning. Someone who is ordinarily a guiding leader may have to adopt a directing style in emergency situations, for example, just as a directing leader might shift to an enabling style when faced with unanimity of opinion among staff. Favoring a certain leadership style, then, does not make that style static or unchanging (Northouse, 2015).

Shifts in Leadership Styles: Case Studies

The following case studies show how leadership styles can shift to better address different situations. Read each one and then answer the questions that follow.

Case Study A

Jessica was enthusiastic about her fourth year serving as the lead of the school's math department. Her colleagues were friendly, and she felt they always supported her decisions. One year, a new block schedule was in effect that featured a double math period to accommodate the district mandate that students complete an additional year of math instruction before graduation. When the principal told Jessica about this change, she was hesitant at first but figured her department could handle it.

During the first math department meeting of the year, Jessica was surprised to hear the other math teachers complain that they hadn't been consulted in advance about the new block schedule. Lesson plans needed to be adjusted as the curriculum was originally built for shorter, more traditional class periods. The complaints frustrated Jessica, who knew her teachers were capable of implementing the new schedule—and she made her frustration known at the meeting. "I don't really care what you think about the new block schedule," she said. "It is what it is, and we have to do it. Case closed."

Case Study A Questions

1. *What leadership style(s) does Jessica display?*

_____

_____

2. *What evidence do you have to support each style?*

_____

_____

_____

3. *What leadership style do you think would be best in this situation? How could Jessica have employed that style?*

_____

_____

_____

Case Study B

Brian prided himself on empowering his staff to make their own decisions about student learning. During a recent classroom walkthrough, Brian noticed that students were loud, unengaged, and socializing during the middle of class. The teacher, Michael, was sitting at his desk typing on his laptop. When Brian approached him to ask what the plan for that day was, Michael answered that students were engaging in "work time" that didn't require him to teach or lead discussions. This response bothered Brian, who felt that a lot of potential instructional time was being wasted, but he wasn't sure whether he should step in and tell Michael to teach more or keep quiet and trust Michael's judgment.

Case Study B Questions

1. *What leadership style(s) does Brian display?*

_____

_____

2. *What evidence do you have to support each style?*

_____

_____

_____

3. *What leadership style do you think would be best in this situation? How could Brian have employed that style?*

_____

_____

_____

Case Study C

Recently, there was a dispute on the school board. One board member was pushing to allocate funds for a new stadium while another was advocating for a salary increase for teachers. Nicole, the school principal, knew both matters were important, but other educators quickly took sides and Nicole could feel the tension building in her school. A small argument erupted into a pushing and shoving match at the last staff meeting, when a history teacher (and parent of a star athlete) took offense at a math teacher's comment that all the school cared about was sports. Several teachers intervened as Nicole struggled to gain her composure. Rather than address the conflict, she told both teachers she wanted to see them first thing the next morning.

Case Study C Questions

1. *What leadership style(s) does Nicole display?*

_____

_____

2. *What evidence do you have to support each style?*

_____

_____

_____

3. *What leadership style do you think would be best in this situation? How could Nicole have employed that style?*

_____

_____

_____

Assessment: What Is Your Leadership Style?

Completing a leadership inventory and understanding your own personal leadership style is an important step in developing your PLP. Read the following statements, circling the numbers of those that you believe reflect your own leadership. When you are done, the section with the most items selected will correspond to your preferred leadership style (or styles).

Directing Leadership Style

1. I continually supervise my staff to ensure they complete their work.
2. I think staff are generally lazy or don't take responsibility for their work.
3. I think staff must be given rewards or punishments in order to stay motivated.
4. I think my staff rely on my opinion to feel secure in their job or to gain approval for their work.
5. I am the person who is ultimately responsible for the achievements or failures of staff.

Guiding Leadership Style

1. I allow staff to be part of the decision-making process.
2. I provide guidance or advice to staff without pressuring them to do things my way.
3. I frequently communicate my support to staff.
4. I try to help my staff set their own goals.
5. I like to help staff members find their passion.

Enabling Leadership Style

1. In complex situations, I let staff work problems out on their own.
2. I try to stay out of the way of staff as they do their work.
3. I think staff are the best judges of their own work.

4. I give staff complete freedom to solve problems on their own.

5. In most situations, staff request little input from me and make decisions on their own.

Instructional Leadership Style

1. I have up-to-date knowledge of curriculum, instruction, and student assessment practices.

2. I provide staff with instructional resources related to instruction and assessment.

3. Staff would say I empower those around me, promote collegiality, and can be trusted.

4. I am a competent planner. I am able to identify goals, recognize changes that need to occur, observe my environment, and involve the appropriate people in the decision-making process.

5. I feel comfortable delivering feedback to help create an effective learning environment.

Servant Leadership Style

1. I always put staff first, even if it involves self-sacrifice.

2. I am sensitive to the personal concerns of staff.

3. I help staff grow and succeed by empowering them to autonomously decide when and how to complete their own tasks.

4. I have high moral standards and act with moral integrity.

5. I feel most comfortable engaging with staff at the interpersonal level.

Reflecting on Your Results

1. *Do you feel your results are accurate? Why or why not?*

_____

_____

_____

2. Which statement made you feel conflicted about whether it fit you? Why?

_____

_____

_____

_____

_____

_____

3. Did any statements cause you to think of different colleagues or situations you've encountered in your job? Why do you think that is?

_____

_____

_____

_____

_____

_____

4. What surprised you most about the assessment?

_____

_____

_____

_____

_____

_____

5. *Were you disappointed by any results? If so, which ones? Why do you think these are the results you got?*

_____

_____

_____

_____

_____

6. *Which leadership style feels the most comfortable to you? Which style causes you to feel discomfort? Why do you think this is?*

_____

_____

_____

_____

_____

Conclusion

Part of the beauty of leadership is that there is no one "right" leadership style and we can learn to use different styles at different times. As we gain more knowledge about how to better support students and teachers, our leadership roles evolve. In decades past, school leaders were often relegated to administrative tasks such as budgeting and supply orders. By contrast, today's school leaders are charged with cultivating emotionally supportive environments where students can thrive—a responsibility that rarely keeps them in their offices for long and most often finds them working closely alongside teachers and building relationships with the school community.

Leadership roles in schools tend to allow for a wide diversity of styles. What works for one school leader may not work for you, and that is completely appropriate (and even expected). What matters is that you understand and can articulate your leadership style so others know what to expect from you and so you can evaluate your own consistency in leadership over time. You may aspire to be a guiding or transformational leader, but your assessment results may place you in the directing column. Now you have the opportunity to figure out how to move from one to another.

Bradley Smith wrote about the importance of a school leader being able to identify his or her leadership style. "When you step into a school," he wrote, "the culture of the school is immediately evident and is a major indicator of the efficiency of the school. . . . School leaders are critical in guiding these values, beliefs and behaviors of their school" (2016, p. 71). He noted that in schools where transformational leaders were in charge, teachers were more driven and more satisfied with their jobs.

If you are unwilling or unable to identify your leadership style, how will you articulate your decision-making processes to the school board? How will parents be able to understand why your decisions might look and feel different for each student? How confident will teachers be in their own decision-making processes? Knowing, owning, and sharing your leadership style is one aspect of explaining how and why you lead the way you do.

Reflective Questions

Think about leaders you have known in your lifetime. Identify by name someone who has demonstrated each of the following leadership styles:

- Directing: _____
- Guiding: _____

- Enabling: _____
- Instructional: _____
- Servant: _____

Reflection Questions

1. What made each leader you listed effective or ineffective?
2. Which leader strikes you as worth emulating?
3. How did followers respond to each leader's style? What did you notice the most?
4. What leadership style do you feel you need to exhibit to get your job done?
5. What (if anything) surprised you about the preferred leadership style or styles that emerged during the assessment exercise in this chapter?
6. When do you feel like your leadership style might be seen as a weakness? Why?
7. What assumptions do people make about you because of your title that are inconsistent with your leadership style? How can you go about changing some of those assumptions?
8. Do you ever have to use a leadership style that isn't natural to you? If so, when? How can you make that style feel more natural to you, even if just for a few moments?

Leadership Style: Additional Resources

- **CliftonStrengths:** A personality assessment that measures your strengths. (www.gallup.com/cliftonstrengths/en/252137/home.aspx)
- **Myers-Briggs Type Indicator:** A personality inventory that identifies how people perceive the world and make decisions by categorizing

their personality into 16 distinct groups. (www.myersbriggs.org/my-mbti-personality-type/take-the-mbti-instrument)

- **Emotional Intelligence:** An assessment to determine your level of emotional intelligence. (www.mindtools.com/pages/article/ei-quiz.htm)
- **Blind Spot Assessment:** An assessment that identifies your blind spots, which can influence your decision making and leadership behaviors. (https://ww3.blindspots.com/bsa)

4

What Are My
Core Values?

Connie was ending her 23rd year as an elementary school princi-
pal in a small coastal town where school pride ran deep from genera-
tion to generation. During her time at the school, Connie had grown
accustomed to seeing her former students grow into the parents of her
current students. These generations of students lauded Connie for her
willingness to serve, her innovation and creativity, and her passion
for students.

Even though Connie appreciated the constant support, she also
felt like she had lost her way. Recent retirements of trusted colleagues,
battles with the school board over reduced funding for classrooms, and
a steady feeling of burnout plagued her. She knew she was nowhere
near retirement and she really did not want to leave her job, but she
felt unsettled and confused as to where she was really headed. After
all, where is a late-career former kindergarten teacher going to go?
As she strolled the halls of the school one day, listening to the steady

hum of student learning, teacher chatter, and playground laughter, Connie thought about why she entered teaching in the first place: her passion for growth and her desire to serve. What did these values mean to her today?

Leadership styles have plenty of utility, but they do not capture the how and why of who you are or what you value in your school. In the vignette above, Connie had lost touch with her core values—something that is easy to do when we don't examine those values regularly and with care. Because of this, she struggled internally, wondering if she was even meant to be in education.

Core values are beliefs and qualities that tend to be nonnegotiable and remain consistent over time, such as honesty, responsibility, and trust. They are traits that an individual considers to be important, are relatively stable over time, and affect mindset and behavior regardless of position or title (Daft, 2015). All school leaders have certain core values on which they will not compromise. For example, most school leaders will attest to the need for trust and open communication with teachers, students, parents, and community members. Other leaders might identify a heavy sense of responsibility as a core value. Yet others might identify compassion, leading them to focus on securing more resources for struggling students or on the well-being of their teaching staff.

Core values can be individual or tied to the entire school community. Consider the mottos you see printed in school handbooks or painted on the entrance walls of school buildings: "Respect Others," "Celebrate Diversity," "Work Hard, Play Hard." These statements succinctly telegraph a school's core values—we use them to facilitate community conversations, guide behaviors, create a collective identity, and work together toward a common mission.

As school leaders, core values guide our decision making and help us stay centered on what we believe to be the most important and fundamental principles in life. Whether we recognize it or not, we are constantly valuing things, people, or ideas as good or bad, ethical or unethical, favorable or unfavorable (Daft, 2015). Ethics and values can alter the way we perceive and react to stimuli. For example, someone with a high regard for collaboration will tend to engage in behaviors such as including all team members in decisions, sharing information as it relates to team goals, and making sure everyone's ideas are considered. By the same token, individuals who value compassion will invest in others by establishing deep connections, exhibiting empathy, and helping to fill others' unmet needs. Identifying our core values can help us decide our course of action as situations arise (Carr, 2013). We turn to these values when we feel unsettled, disjointed, or unsure of which direction to go.

Consider This

Jamison worked as a school superintendent for nearly five years. In that time, he had overseen the construction of new buildings, the influx of hundreds of students, and the implementation of a new technology initiative. At a recent school board meeting, Jamison was challenged by a new board member who alleged that Jamison purchased an online curriculum package for the new one-to-one initiative based on a personal connection he had with the sales representative. The problem, it appeared, was that Jamison's cousin worked as a vendor selling the curriculum that the district purchased. Jamison knew that the curriculum was the right fit for the students in the district and was confident his cousin's role in selling the product had no influence. However, it did give the appearance that perhaps Jamison, who prided himself on honesty and transparency, may be exercising judgment in contradiction of that.

What core values would someone in Jamison's position be expected to practice?

_____

_____

_____

_____

_____

If you were on the school board, would you question Jamison's purchase of the online curriculum? Why or why not?

_____

_____

_____

_____

_____

Did Jamison's core values conflict with what you believe the role of school leader to be? Why or why not?

_____

_____

_____

_____

_____

8

Was Jamison wrong for doing what he did? Why or why not?

_____

_____

_____

_____

Should Jamison be trusted?

_____

_____

_____

_____

As Jamison's example shows, following our core values is not always easy and may not always yield an ideal result, especially when held up to the light of public criticism. Very often, however, these values can guide us in the right direction, as many school leaders' actions during the COVID-19 pandemic showed. For example, MSNBC reported on one Detroit principal, Jacqueline Dungey, who told stories of how her students suddenly went missing when they weren't required to show up at school every day. Rather than shrug her shoulders or blame others, Dungey activated her core values and began to seek out her missing students, focusing on those who most needed social supports, community resources, and the structure of the school system. As she said about one of the students she worked to find, "I just wanted to make sure he was safe" (Einhorn,

Consider This

When the COVID-19 pandemic shuttered schools across the country, what priorities did you witness being weighed against one another? How did school leaders, teachers, parents, community members, and politicians describe the role of schools and teachers? Did any of these descriptions minimize the role of schools today? What takeaways could you ascertain about the roles of teachers and school leaders? How did these takeaways make you feel?

_____

_____

_____

_____

_____

_____

2020, para. 5). In this example, one of Dungey's core values—the need to protect and secure safety for her students—rose above the rest.

Core values are really what drive us to excel at what we do—they form the foundation that encourages others to trust and follow us. When decisions need to be made, whether they are about the hiring or firing of teachers, the allocation of money within a budget, or laying out a new school schedule, they affect the overall perception of the school leader—and, in turn, the trust placed in him or her. Perceived "good" decisions might build public confidence and secure enthusiasm from a school board, whereas perceived "bad" decisions might foster questions of incompetence or suitability for the job. Core values, then, are what help us feel secure in whatever decision we make—that we know, in our hearts and minds, that we are doing what is best for our school.

Core values remind us of some of the most rewarding aspects of working in schools. We love the story of Nebraska teacher Trey Payne, who walked into his classroom one day to discover his personal gym bag had been opened and his pair of expensive tennis shoes had been stolen. Payne told students that whoever took the shoes could return them, no questions asked. The shoes did return, but in an unexpected way: a video that went viral nationwide showed Payne's students pooling money to purchase a new pair of shoes for him. Why did they do it? They said it was because of the core values Payne demonstrated in class with them every day: trust, respect, and care for his students no matter what they did and who they were. They said they wanted to repay him for how he treated them all year by replacing his shoes (Ebrahimji, 2020). Clearly, our core values can have an enormous impact on others.

School principal Rita Platt wrote about how she works through decision-making processes by examining her core values: "I have learned over many years (49 to be specific) of trial and error that I feel best when I have clarity about the reasons behind my decisions. Knowing my core values helps me not only to make decisions but also, and perhaps more importantly, to determine the reasons I am making them" (Platt, 2018, para 15). Platt reviews her core values daily to ensure her leadership choices always align with them.

Our core values are often ideals we might struggle to implement without flaws, but they remain central to who we are. Consider the core value of "responsibility," which we know many school leaders consider most important of all. With this one core value come other related issues, such as the duty to care for others, the weight of decision making, and the ability to stand alone when others criticize you. Responsibility can be a tremendous opportunity to demonstrate commitment, but it can also lead to uncertainty and indecision. In this way, our core values, necessary though they are, can serve as both gift and curse.

Assessment: Identifying Your Core Values

Recognizing and naming your core values will facilitate conversation in your school community and allow you to understand why your decision-making process may differ from others'. Take time to thoroughly read the list of values in Figure 4.1. This assessment divides core values into two categories: core values that influence your behavior and core values that influence your thinking. Some of these core values may overlap, yet others may be values you find irrelevant to your role as school leader. This assessment is designed to ensure you must make difficult choices and eliminate lukewarm responses. Consider which core values, from whichever list, you think are truly nonnegotiable in your role as a school leader, then circle the three you feel are most important to you. If a core value with which you identify is not listed, feel free to add it to the list. Answer honestly and don't rely on the input of others to sway your choices. As school leaders, it is incredibly important for you to be able to articulate your core values. (It's possible that you'll find everything on the lists important; very few, after all, will find no value in honesty, selflessness, or understanding. Nevertheless, selecting three will help you prioritize and can clarify the choices for you when you face tough decisions as a leader.)

FIGURE 4.1
Leadership Values

Core Values That Influence Behaviors	Core Values That Influence Thinking
Acceptance	Autonomy
Accountability	Bravery
Collaboration	Commitment
Commitment	Consistency
Common Sense	Curiosity
Dedication	Encouragement
Dependability	Excellence
Diligence	Exploration
Fairness	Flexibility
Humility	Honesty
Innovation	Independence
Kindness	Motivation
Loyalty	Openness
Open-mindedness	Partnership
Performance	Passion
Power	Perseverance
Professionalism	Productiveness
Reliability	Resilience
Respect	Resourcefulness
Self-control	Solidarity
Selflessness	Vision
Support	Willingness to Learn
Trustworthiness	*Other:*
Understanding	
Willingness to Take Risks	
Other:	

Now, for the three values you've identified as most important to you, answer the following questions.

Core Value 1:

1. *Why is this value important to you?*

_____

_____

_____

_____

_____

2. *When have you used/demonstrated/exhibited this core value in your work?*

_____

_____

_____

_____

_____

Core Value 2:

1. *Why is this value important to you?*

_____

_____

_____

_____

_____

2. *When have you used/demonstrated/exhibited this core value in your work?*

_____

_____

_____

_____

Core Value 3:

1. *Why is this value important to you?*

_____

_____

_____

_____

2. *When have you used/demonstrated/exhibited this core value in your work?*

_____

_____

_____

_____

Assessment in Action

Monica, an elementary school principal, completed the assessment above and identified her core values as calmness, loyalty, and stability. Her staff agreed that she exhibited these values when making decisions. Indeed, she was great at her job.

One year, Monica was asked to move to a different school and replace a principal who had unexpectedly quit halfway through the school year. She was torn. Her core values called her to stay in one place, be a stable presence for her teachers, and not jump positions in the middle of the year. District leadership heavily leaned on Monica to make the move, knowing her leadership was just what this school needed.

After giving it thought, Monica ended up declining the move. "My teachers and students depend on me to be here," she said. "When we started the year, I said I would be here from the first day to the last, and I can't go back on that commitment."

Monica's core values were central to her identity as a school leader. Though some might argue that she lost an opportunity for advancement or a new chapter in her career, Monica knew that, by acting in accordance with her core values, she had made the right decision for her and her school community.

When Core Values Are Challenged

Sometimes circumstances require us to go against our core values, which can cause us to wonder how essential they were in the first place. Think about the school principal who must reduce the number of teachers in a school but whose core values include loyalty and compassion. Since the cuts must be made regardless, both the principal and staff might come to doubt how deeply held those values ever were.

The key point about core values is that they are the center of our decision-making processes, so when our core values are challenged, we often seek advice from others in similar circumstances, rethink our decision-making analyses, and contemplate the potential results of our decisions. Difficult decisions are a part of every job, but these decisions need not be a measure of the leader's worth. Having to make decisions that seem contrary to one's core values does not mean the core values do not exist; rather, in this particular circumstance, other external factors may be more important.

The alleged perception of our decisions is an unreliable method on which to base our decision-making processes. Instead, we should rely on the objective facts that influence how and why we make decisions. Making a decision that seems to conflict with your core values does not mean your decision is bad—it means you engaged in a deliberate process to do what is best for your school community. Although we may feel the pull of our core values being challenged, we can still be true to those values and make sound decisions for our school.

Integrating Core Values into Our Practice

Core values help keep us centered and grounded in our work. As Patrick Lencioni (2002) writes, leaders should "weave core values into everything." For educators, this means integrating them into every aspect of the school community, from hiring practices to school routines to staff meetings to website design. In doing this, leaders help strengthen the entire organization while also ensuring that all aspects of it are aligned to the same principles.

Of course, our core values will not always be in complete harmony with the requirements of leadership. The following case studies show examples of educators navigating conflicts between their core values and school-based decisions. Read each one and then answer the corresponding questions.

Case Study A

Jeremy serves as an instructional leader at a K–5 school. His daily work involves coaching teachers, managing assessment processes, and meeting with other school leaders to identify gaps in the school's instructional processes. When it was time for state testing, Jeremy anticipated a huge gap in the math test scores for this year's 5th grade class. Last year, their teacher had failed to implement the school's curriculum, and the class was constantly behind peer groups in the assessment data he collected.

As part of his leadership training, Jeremy identified his core values as integrity, vision, and success. Poor scores from his 5th graders could mean the school would lose the funding needed to hire a new teacher next year. Jeremy considered approaching the math teacher with specific instructions to "teach to the test," which he knew would go against his core value of integrity. Jeremy knew "teaching to the test" might increase test scores, but students would lose valuable experiential learning as a result. His integrity pushed him to ignore the pressure being put on him for increasing test scores, but his desire for success still made him consider pushing the teacher to stick to the content covered on the test.

Case Study A Questions

1. *Given Jeremy's core values, what should he do and why?*

_____

_____

_____

_____

_____

2. *What factors should Jeremy consider when making his decision?*

_____

_____

_____

_____

_____

3. *What are the risks and rewards of following one core value over another in this situation?*

_____

_____

_____

_____

_____

Case Study B

Anne is a veteran high school principal working in a suburban district at a school with more than 2,000 students. Julie, an English teacher, recently wrote a disciplinary report on a student, Jackson, for some sexually suggestive remarks he had made to her during class.

Anne knew Jackson to be relatively outgoing and friendly. She had also worked with Jackson's mom in the school district and had graduated from high school with Jackson's dad. She had a hard time imagining that the intent behind his comments were meant to be harassing, yet she had no doubt that Julie sincerely perceived them as such. Anne struggled with how to best support Julie while also upholding her core values of fairness and consistency. After all, she valued her relationship with Jackson and his family and did not want to ruin her long-term relationships, but she also wanted Julie to feel heard and valued.

Case Study B Questions

1. *Given Anne's core values, what should she do and why?*

_____

_____

_____

_____

_____

2. *What factors should Anne consider when making her decision?*

_____

_____

_____

_____

_____

3. *What are the risks and rewards of following one core value over another in this situation?*

_____

_____

_____

_____

_____

Case Study C

Carter is an elementary school principal at a school with a high percentage of special needs and special education students. One of his 6th grade students, Doug, is on the autism spectrum and exhibits behavior disorders. Most days end with Doug facing some sort of discipline due to an outburst or physical attacks on teachers or other students. Today, Carter had to intervene as Doug was punching and scratching his daily para-helper, Mrs. Allen. He pulled Doug's body off Mrs. Allen, who then ran out of the room in tears.

Carter knew he needed to balance protecting his teachers with meeting the needs of his students. His core values of inclusiveness, fairness, and compassion only guided him to sympathize with the plight of each side, and he was unsure how best to proceed.

Case Study C Questions

1. *Given Carter's core values, what should he do and why?*

_____

_____

_____

_____

_____

2. *What factors should Carter consider when making his decision?*

_____

_____

_____

_____

_____

3. *What are the risks and rewards of following one core value over another in this situation?*

_____

_____

_____

_____

Reflection Questions

1. What surprised you about your top core values?

2. In the assessment, which of the core values were you forced to eliminate? Which were most difficult to discard? What rationale allowed you to delete those from your final list?

3. Think of a time when you had to make a value-based decision. What was it and how did you know the decision was value-based?

4. What core values do you feel are important to your colleagues at school? How do you know?

5. How do others in school know your core values? In what ways do you demonstrate these values? How can you get better at demonstrating them?

6. What core values do people think you have simply because of your title? How are your identified values the same as or different than these perceived values?

7. How can you communicate your core values with your school community while also acknowledging the different core values held by others?

Core Values: Additional Resources

- **Personal Values Assessment:** A survey that provides information about why you do what you do, based on your personal values. (www.valuescentre.com/tools-assessments/pva)
- **Cultural Design for Positive School Learning Environments:** This website is specifically designed to help school communities build and live core values. (https://gotcorevalues.com/school-leaders-educators)

5

What Is My Mindset?

Andrea landed her dream job as a high school principal at the beginning of last school year. Prior to earning her administrative degree, she taught music in the same building she was hired to lead. Andrea was a compassionate, consistent leader who was present at nearly all school events and maintained an open-door policy for her staff. Though she prided herself on being accessible, her constant availability caused her to fall behind on teacher evaluations, disciplinary record keeping, and parent phone calls.

As the weeks wore on, Andrea started to breeze right past her office staff and shut her office door. She became tired and irritable. She knew she needed to regroup somehow, but the days just kept dragging on and her exhaustion became apparent in the dark circles under her eyes and her slumped shoulders. As teachers approached her with classroom management issues, she began wondering why they couldn't just handle the problems themselves. When parents called, she avoided answering the phone. Though she maintained her presence at school events, it was entirely physical—not emotional.

Andrea never expected the job to be this exhausting or wearing. Soon, staff became irritable and conflicts began to emerge over minor issues like classroom space and access to resources. Andrea began to wonder if her mindset was contagious. If so, what could she do about it? How could she become the leader she dreamt of being?

Our mindset can change throughout the day depending on interactions with others, conversations in the hallways, or personal well-being issues. It is a culmination of our attitudes, our beliefs about success and failure, and our perception of the ability and talent around us. A school community can view, critique, and assess its leaders' commitment, leadership style, and capability simply by gauging their mindset.

Within the framework of studying our everyday reactions to the events around us, we tend to embrace or exhibit one of two "mindsets" or beliefs about our own ability to approach a situation: a growth mindset or a fixed mindset. Stanford psychologist Carol Dweck spent much of her career laying out this framework based on three decades of research. In this research, she clearly defined both types of mindsets. Her work, then, investigated how when one embraces a specific type of mindset, that person's approach to learning, new opportunities, and even decision making is influenced.

A fixed mindset is one where you believe the traits, talents, and skills you have are unable to be changed; they are "carved in stone" (Dweck, 2016, p. 6). When we have a fixed mindset, we often try to prove to others that we are talented or skilled at something—because, after all, we only have a certain amount of intelligence, talent, or skill. Those with a fixed mindset tend to avoid taking risks because it may lead to failure. They also tend to engage in negative self-talk (e.g., "I'll never be good at this," "I feel dumb"). Consequently, they develop an aversion to making waves by trying new things.

A growth mindset, on the other hand, is based on the belief that you can learn, grow, and evolve. It embraces the idea that one's potential is unknown, so with hard work and persistence, much can be accomplished. Those with a growth mindset are willing to seek challenges, take risks, and fail because they recognize that they learn something from the experience. Over time, as you experience life and learn new things, you grow   and that is embraced within the growth mindset.

Within education, we hear a lot about the benefit of the growth mindset. It makes sense that in a place of learning, such as a school, being open to new ideas, problem solving, critical thinking, and failing are part of the daily processes of acquiring and understanding new content. Students who exhibit a growth mindset learn more; more importantly, they strive to learn more. By contrast, students with a fixed mindset tend to believe their learning capacity is limited or that working harder really won't have any payoff.

The same is true for school leaders. Those who believe things will never change—that their influence is minimal at best and that the status quo is better than trying to innovate and improve—are leading from a fixed mindset. This can lead to shallow relationships, a culture in which challenge is not embraced, and leaders who make the same decisions year after year without considering the changing needs of the school. Those who embrace a growth mindset are innovative, willing to invest in meaningful relationships, and willing to try new decision-making approaches, even if they don't always go perfectly.

It can be hard for school leaders to develop a growth mindset when so much responsibility rests on their shoulders, but it is crucial to innovation and change. Through our words and actions, our mindset can demonstrate to students and teachers that learning can be both challenging and rewarding and that part of the learning process is learning from our failures.

Most of us are probably not used to having our mindset scrutinized by those around us. In fact, we probably just assume our mindset is a natural, unremarkable reaction to what happens during the course of the day. However, as leaders, we need to acknowledge the impact of our mindset on both our school community and our own well-being. Think through the variety of situations you face in a day. Where do you feel constrained? Where do you fear risk taking? When are you exhibiting a fixed mindset? Do others admire you for your outlook, or are you the pessimist others avoid? How does being a leader affect your mindset and how others perceive you? Keep the following in mind. Those with a fixed mindset

- Avoid risk.
- Believe they have a set amount of talent or skill.
- Think that trying hard will not produce results.
- Are not open to feedback (and when feedback is present, ignore it or take it as personal criticism).
- Seem intimidated by others' success.
- Seek to hide weaknesses.

Your mindset affects more than just you. When the teachers and students you work alongside every day fear failing or disappointing you, a fixed mindset is at play. Though it may be comfortable and predictable, a fixed mindset can also be stifling. As a leader, it is important to understand that a fixed mindset is not necessarily a fault; rather, it is a way of avoiding risk. By contrast, those with a growth mindset

- Set a productive and encouraging tone for teachers.
- Promote learning-centered expectations for students.
- Encourage a schoolwide culture of learning.
- Facilitate innovation and creative thinking.
- Help develop strong relationships and partnerships.
- Support collaboration among different types of learners and teachers.
- Address the social and emotional needs of learners.
- Accept failure as a necessary part of learning.
- Enable functional resolutions to conflicts.

Put simply, your mindset as a school leader is critical to motivating others and promoting well-being among students and staff. Struggling to embrace a growth mindset is like refusing to look in a mirror before taking part in a fashion show—you may convince yourself you are put together, but that's probably not how the world sees you.

Mindset, Burnout, and Turnover

A fixed mindset, or struggling to embrace change and development, can also lead to burnout. The condition of burnout is described as being "exhausted, cynical, and hostile towards one's work, and down on one's job performance" (Khazan, 2021, para. 4). Psychoanalyst Herbert Freudenberger coined the word *burnout* in the 1970s to describe the effect of constant stress that eventually leads to a loss of passion, motivation, and increasing cynicism, which occurs in highly dedicated professionals (Michel, 2016). Freudenberger (1980) defined a person experiencing burnout as "someone in a state of fatigue or frustration brought about by devotion to a cause, way of life, or relationship that failed to produce the expected reward" (p. 13). The World Health Organization classified burnout as an "occupational phenomenon" in 2019. In its definition, it characterized three attributes of burnout: (1) feelings of exhaustion, (2) increased emotional or mental distance from one's professional role, and (3) reduced professional effectiveness (World Health Organization, 2019).

Burnout, then, is not a sign of weakness or lack of skill. Burnout is about not having enough—that is, not enough emotional or physical resources to cope with your life. When we experience burnout, we feel empty, exhausted, and unmotivated instead of fulfilled, passionate, and invigorated. We lack time, information, feedback, meaningful recognition, and control. It is a result of exceptional dedication to a job, relationship, or process that we believe in so fully that we work ourselves into a state of exhaustion—so much so that we end up distancing ourselves from our work, friends, and family and are left wondering where our passion was extinguished along the way.

For school leaders, burnout emerges over time through an extended exposure to the daily stressors of the job, which add up and wear away at one's professional drive. Over time, the school leader becomes exhausted, tired of fighting, and begins to wonder if he or she is actually making a difference. That feeling becomes persistent and then leads to futile attempts to manage the out-of-control feelings; often, these management techniques lead to quick fixes like substance abuse, avoiding others, escaping difficult conversations, and dissatisfaction in our everyday lives. Rather than resolve the burnout, these quick fixes can lead to depression and isolation.

Symptoms of Burnout

Unlike many physical ailments, burnout can manifest over the course of time and in many different ways. Consider some of these symptoms of burnout:

- Exhaustion
- Boredom
- Detachment
- Paranoia
- Depression
- Chronic Fatigue
- Physical Ailments (e.g., headaches, stomach issues)
- Impatience
- Irritability
- Loss of Passion

Burnout does not go away at the end of a school year or by changing one's job. Instead, it is a lingering condition that, over time, expands and takes over one's perception and beliefs about others and the world around them. Instead of feeling goal-oriented, one may begin to wonder if their talent or intelligence is actually a fraud. Rather than feeling energetic at the beginning of a day, one begins to dread what lies ahead. Additionally, burnout may look different from person to person. In other words, what you experience as burnout may be completely different from what someone else does. However, the main theme is that burnout leads to feelings of hopelessness and a sense of a loss of control. For those in leadership positions, who are used to being relied on and seen as pillars of security, this can be a difficult condition in which to live.

Why Burnout Affects School Leaders

One interesting attribute of burnout is that it tends to affect high achievers the most. This includes goal-oriented, career-driven, ambitious professionals who are often in fields dedicated to helping others. In fact, Freudenberger (1980) wrote about the people who fall prey to burnout:

> (They) are decent individuals who have striven hard to reach a goal. Their schedules are busy, and whatever the project or job, they can be counted on to do more than their share. They're usually the leaders among us who have never been able to admit to limitations. They're burning out because they've pushed themselves too hard for too long. They started out with great expectations and refused to compromise along the way. (pp. 11–12)

School leaders, it seems, are prime candidates for burnout and eventual turnover. The average tenure of a principal is about four years, and the turnover rate of principals is about 18 percent nationally (Levin, Scott, Yang, Leung, & Bradley, 2020). In 2020, a National Association of Secondary School Principals (NASSP) survey of school principals found that 42 percent were considering leaving the position due to such factors as challenging working conditions, compensation unequal to the workload, a lack of decision-making authority, and lack of institutional support for professional development. If we want our school leaders to have longevity in their roles, we must consider how the conditions of the job are affecting the physical and emotional well-being of the people serving in those roles.

Case Study

Taylor is in her fourth year as an elementary school principal. Through the course of this school year, she found herself slowly detaching from her job. Conflicts with students' parents, a hiring freeze leaving a lack of qualified teachers available for overfilled classrooms, and a growing pile of paperwork on her desk made every day seem unapproachable and unpredictable. She started to feel dread on her drive to school every day. At the end of a long work day, she would pick up fast food on the way home because she knew she did not want to cook dinner. It was common for Taylor to unwind with a glass of wine (or several) and get lost scrolling through social media. Her once strong passion for working with students was now lost in mundane tasks and repetitive conflicts. She started to gain weight, detach from her personal relationships, and struggle to maintain attention while at work.

Case Study Questions

1. *What facets of Taylor's job are leading her to stress and potential burnout?*

_____

_____

2. *What do you think causes Taylor to feel this way?*

_____

_____

3. *If Taylor were to embrace a growth mindset, what might change about how she reacts to conditions of her job?*

_____

_____

The spring of 2020 introduced a new slate of challenges to school leader well-being related to the shift to remote learning and the shuttering of schools as a result of the COVID-19 pandemic. That year, 45 percent of principals reported that pandemic working conditions were accelerating their plans to leave the profession (Farrace, 2020). According to JoAnn Bartoletti, executive director and CEO of the NASSP,

> These new findings on principals' departure plans should frighten the entire education community. Our schools are already strained by principal turnover, and the school conditions policymakers have created will only intensify that turnover. Couple that reality with a shallowed pool of future principals caused by teacher layoffs and attrition, and we have a full-blown crisis in finding talented educators to lead our schools. We must make it a priority to attend to the needs of current principals and continue efforts to deepen the bench of leadership talent. (Farrace, 2020, para 3)

Each year, it seems, a new stressor lands at the feet of school leaders and educators. Class sizes increase, professional development becomes more complex and expensive, students' emotional and social needs rise, and public opinions get louder and more divisive. It is no wonder that the turnover rate is increasing rapidly, especially when so many school leaders were unprepared for their roles from the start. Unfortunately, turnover due to burnout leaves many schools filling leadership positions with those willing to serve regardless of how well they understand the complexities of leadership.

No one can manage your mindset and potential for burnout except you. Even though we tend to want to focus on how others treat us, why others say certain things to us, or how others perceive us, in reality, our beliefs about our own talent, potential, and impact is within our control. Although others might influence it, at the end of the day, you are the only person who can decide how you will respond to a situation or an individual. Within the school setting, you are inevitably barraged with external influences, from students to teachers to budgets to basketball games, but how you handle these external influences—by internalizing the challenges as personal faults or recognizing opportunities for influencing others—is entirely up to you.

Consider This

The turnover rate among school leaders can cause serious disruption to school communities. List the top three stressors you face related to your job today. Then identify two to three specific actions you can take today to address them.

Example:

Stressor: My work life is out of balance. I am answering emails until 11:00 p.m. and wake up to answer more at 5:30 a.m. I struggle to shut my mind down when I know my inbox is filling up.

Action Item #1: I can begin to eat a healthier menu, bringing lunch to work and identifying food that provides sustained energy rather than a quick high. I can model this practice to my staff and make it a habit.

Action Item #2: I can shut off my phone and computer so I am not constantly interrupted by alerts and alarms. I can place these items in my work bag so I do not drag them out before my workday begins.

Stressor:

_____

_____

_____

Action Item #1:

_____

_____

_____

Action Item #2:

_____

_____

_____

Traits of Leaders with a Growth Mindset

This list provides some constructive, practical ways you can take action and manage your mindset every day in your school community. Leaders who embrace a growth mindset

- Seek out professional development that promotes a growth mindset. Attend learning opportunities you wouldn't normally sign up for. Learn new skills and expand your knowledge about areas that are unfamiliar to you. Demonstrate a willingness to learn, fail, and try new things.

- Develop a network of other local school leaders who understand the daily challenges. They are also available to listen to others in their network and can serve as a sounding board when their peers feel their mindset becoming fixed.

- Engage in purposeful human interaction, for example, by making it their aim to participate in one positive student interaction per class period or to conduct informal walkthroughs, which let them see the positive, innovative work going on in their buildings.

- Practice positive self-talk. Shockingly, according to Cathy Lassiter (2017), 95 percent of a school leader's self-talk is negative (p. 2). These leaders monitor their self-talk and stop negative self-talk as soon as it creeps in.
- Cultivate the community in and around their school. We love this quote from Leyda Garcia, principal of the UCLA Community School in Los Angeles: "What a privilege it is to be a principal. I get all these gifts every day. That's what makes it sustainable" (quoted in Safir, 2019).
- Promote shared responsibility as a practice. They allow teachers and other school leaders to make decisions so they do not become overwhelmed.
- Listen when community members bring their problems but hesitate to offer solutions. Sometimes, being an invested listener empowers the community member to resolve a problem on his or her own.
- Design and participate in leadership coaching opportunities, advocating for leadership training that goes beyond budgets and software to provide mentors, personalized feedback, and opportunities for new school leaders to discuss the realities of their jobs, the personal challenges they face, and well-being practices.

Assessment: Mind Your Mindset

For this exercise, use the chart in Figure 5.1. Think about your day so far (or a recent previous day, if you're completing this in the morning) and circle the emoji that best describes your mindset for each point in the day. Then, in the next column, write one or two words to remind you why your mindset was what it was at this time.

FIGURE 5.1

Mindset Assessment Chart

 Positive Growth Mindset: This is growth mindset at its best: confident; open-minded, open to different opportunities, willing to embrace new opportunities and encounters, and willing to make mistakes in order to learn.

 Moderate Growth Mindset: This level demonstrates a willingness to work hard and an inherent drive to do well. Those with this mindset are open to new ideas and opportunities and have a positive outlook but are hesitant to take risks–yet will do so if evidence supports it.

 Narrow Growth Mindset: This level leans more toward a fixed mindset. Those at this level are willing to promote change but don't want to take the risk when faced with challenges from others. They are not willing to fight to get what they want; in other words, they want learning to be easy, are adverse to failure, and would rather avoid risk than face failure.

 Fixed Mindset: Those with a fixed mindset are unwilling to change, adhering to what is known is the safest choice. They are unwilling to stray from norms or standard procedures, do not want to learn something new, and avoid change because it would mean taking a risk and possibly failing.

Time of Day	Mindset	One- or Two-Word Explanation
Before School	😊 😐 😤 😧	
Arrival Bell	😊 😐 😤 😧	
Mid-morning	😊 😐 😤 😧	
Lunch	😊 😐 😤 😧	
Mid-Afternoon	😊 😐 😤 😧	
Dismissal	😊 😐 😤 😧	
After School	😊 😐 😤 😧	
Evening School Activities	😊 😐 😤 😧	

We acknowledge that emojis are not the most scientific way to keep track of your mindset, but this exercise is meant to help you walk through your day and explore when your mindset might be likeliest to shift. Perhaps your mindset is growth-oriented when students are learning new concepts in class but more fixed when it comes to providing teachers with new choices for professional development. You may begin a day with a growth mindset, excited and ready for a challenge, and end the day with a fixed mindset. It is important to be aware of our mindset and how it might fluctuate throughout our day, given the circumstances we face. By becoming more aware of our mindset, we might be more willing to change it when it does not align with who we want to be as a leader. When we acknowledge we are unwilling to take a risk or face the possibility of failure, we can actively recognize this as a fixed mindset and begin to explore ways to move into the growth mindset.

Consider This

Review your completed mindset chart. For each row, reflect on the following questions:

- *What was my mindset during this time? Fixed or growth? How do I know?*
- *What was influencing my mindset at the time? Was I apt to change my mindset in that moment? Why or why not?*
- *How did my mindset affect others at the time? Did students or others respond to my mindset in a noticeable way?*
- *If I could go back, would I have shifted my mindset? Why or why not?*
- *Overall, how do others perceive my mindset? How can I tell? Does this perception align with the type of mindset I want others to believe that I have? Why or why not?*

How Do I Manage My Mindset?

If your mindset is not where you want it to be, step outside your office or school, find a quiet spot without distraction, shut off your phone, and ask yourself the following questions:

1. *Why do I do this job?*

_____

_____

_____

_____

_____

2. *What do I hope others see in me when doing this job?*

_____

_____

_____

_____

3. *Do I tend to have a fixed or growth mindset? Why?*

_____

_____

_____

_____

_____

4. As a school leader, what do I want others to remember about me?

_____

_____

_____

_____

_____

Sometimes, we must regroup and refocus on what truly matters. If we have a growth mindset and embrace rather than resist hard conversations and challenges, we are more likely to have inner peace about our work— no matter how difficult it may be. During a disciplinary meeting or cafeteria meltdown, we must be able to step back and look at the bigger picture. What brought us into education? Who motivated us to become a teacher or school leader? What did we do today that had a positive effect on someone? With whom did we meaningfully interact today? We must be able to focus not only on the events going on around us but also on the high-quality relationships that support and sustain us.

Consider This

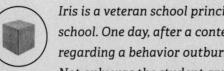

Iris is a veteran school principal in a large urban high school. One day, after a contentious meeting with a student regarding a behavior outburst in class, she felt defeated. Not only was the student argumentative, but the classroom teacher who kicked him out was, too. Iris was caught in the middle again, trying to appease an upset teacher and reluctant to harshly discipline a student who was already on the verge of dropping out of school.

She sat at her desk and thought back on her first few years of teaching and school leadership. Things have gotten more complicated, relationships more difficult, and the promise of changing a student's life trajectory less hopeful than ever. Iris wondered, "Where did I lose my spark for the job? Will I ever be able to regain it?"

1. *What challenges is Iris facing that could influence her mindset toward her job?*

   _____

   _____

   _____

2. *How can Iris best manage the influence of others on her mindset?*

   _____

   _____

   _____

3. *What things can Iris do or say to manage her mindset more effectively?*

   _____

   _____

   _____

Certainly, we have all had days like Iris had—days that make us wonder if education is truly our calling. However, once we recognize and acknowledge this kind of negative mindset creeping in, we can seek to disrupt its progress and change its path.

Consider This

For this activity, find a trusted colleague who knows you well, ask the following questions, and write down what he or she says in the space provided.

1. *Describe my mindset as a school leader in 10 words or less.*

———————————————————————————————

———————————————————————————————

———————————————————————————————

2. *Share a time when my mindset inspired you.*

———————————————————————————————

———————————————————————————————

———————————————————————————————

3. *Share a time when my mindset confused you or caused you to feel negative about our jobs.*

———————————————————————————————

———————————————————————————————

———————————————————————————————

Consider your colleague's responses and reflect on these questions: What makes you feel positive about your role as a school leader? In what way would you rather *not* have your colleague describe you? What can you do to ensure that you are consistently perceived by others as you wish to be perceived?

The 3R Approach to Mindset

We designed the 3R approach to mindset specifically for reflective school leaders. The three *R*s refer to the three steps of recognizing, refocusing, and reenergizing.

Step 1: Recognize. First, we must recognize our mindset. Is it fixed or growth-oriented? Both? Neither? Consider how the chart you completed in Figure 5.1 (p. 71) caused you to stop what you were doing and articulate your frame of mind. You can do something similar on a regular basis. Find a way to monitor yourself throughout the day. Set alarms to regularly track your mindset at different points of your day, using just a few words to remind you why you were in the mindset you were.

Step 2: Refocus. We may not want to believe that our mindset is either fixed or growth-oriented, but it is most likely one or the other at any given point in time. Once you have started to recognize patterns in your mindset, you can purposefully refocus your mindset by reflecting, finding an encouraging work partner, or temporarily moving your attention to a different task.

Step 3: Reenergize. Constantly tracking your mindset can be tiresome, and you may start to find comfort in the idea of keeping it fixed. To remain a productive and inspiring leader, it is imperative that you find ways to reenergize and renew your mindset when this happens. Find an inspirational podcast to listen to on the way to school. Schedule lunch with a group of teachers who can share the challenges and successes in their classrooms. Walk the hallways during passing times simply to connect with students. Often, we find our mindset changes when we surround ourselves with purposeful people—that is, people who are striving to achieve goals, embracing challenges, and sharing learning experiences. Sometimes, it is easy to forget that we are part of that process too and that our work makes an impact. Reenergizing allows us to recognize our importance.

> ### Consider This
>
> *Bart, an award-winning elementary school principal, found that his work was taking a toll on his overall health. Not only did he gain weight from his fast food stops on the way to and from school, but his relationship with his spouse was suffering because he carried the stresses of hungry students and low-achieving teachers home with him. He found his temper short and his exhaustion never-ending. He often fell asleep in the recliner well before his young children went to bed and with the burden of a long to-do list on his mind.*
>
> *Bart considered leaving his leadership job often, for the sake of his physical health and his relationships outside of school. He could also feel that his mindset at school was affecting his support staff, who had begun to complain more about student behavior and lack of resources.*

Overworked, overwhelmed, and on the verge of burnout, Bart sounds like a lot of school leaders. However, the fact that he can link his mindset to his physical and emotional well-being means he can take concrete steps to improve his health, such as taking more walks, focusing on a healthy diet, and meditating. It's easy to overlook, but our overall well-being directly influences how prepared and able we are to face the stresses and successes of the day. Our mindset is directly linked to how prepared we are to face the day and how well we manage what we are asked to face.

Accepting Failure

As we noted earlier in this chapter, a growth mindset helps us accept failure as part of the learning process. New York City school leader Thomas R. Hoerr has this to say about failure and the school leader:

> We need to teach and embrace the term *good failure*. No one wants to fail, but a *good* failure can help us learn and become stronger. Employing the term *good failure* lets everyone know that failing

isn't the end of the world. What matters most is what we do after we fail. With that in mind, we need to go beyond measuring and rewarding students' results and also applaud their effort, trajectory, and progress. (2013, para 6)

Consider This

The traffic jam at Evan's school was a constant headache for him in his role as assistant elementary school principal. Every afternoon was chaotic with children running into traffic, people driving up onto curbs to get around parked cars, and parents arguing with other parents about a myriad of issues. This year, Evan met with his staff to design a new traffic flow for student pickup after school. Instead of allowing cars to drive both directions on the street in front of the school, he worked with local law enforcement to turn the street into a one-way avenue, forcing traffic to flow in a steady manner that allowed for student crosswalks and teacher-led dismissals. Teachers were assigned a specific dismissal spot to monitor and ensure that students were safe and that parents remained in their cars or in a designated pickup spot. The plan seemed flawless.

On the first day of school, as dismissal time approached, Even felt a sense of calmness. He was sure things would go much better than they had in years past. Then, as he walked into the schoolyard, he immediately heard the enraged voices of parents yelling at teachers. He looked into the street and saw cars facing different directions and traffic at a standstill. One parent looked angrily at Evan and yelled, "Who thought up this mess of a plan?!" Evan quickly realized things had gone awry. Parents were mad, teachers were angry, and students were even more confused than usual.

How had this happened, and how had Evan managed to fail so miserably at something so simple?

1. *What evidence is there that Evan had a growth mindset?*

_____

_____

_____

2. *When Evan faced failure, how should he have responded?*

_____

_____

_____

3. *How might Evan better embrace a growth mindset in the face of failure?*

_____

_____

_____

Conclusion

Even the simplest tasks can cause us to slip into a fixed mindset, rather than a growth-oriented one. When we allow fear to overtake us, we remain stuck in old patterns and outdated habits desperately in need of updating. If we expect our teachers and students to solve problems creatively, think strategically, and work collaboratively, we must practice a growth mindset in even our most mundane of daily tasks.

Reflection Questions

1. In what ways does your mindset influence how you approach your day at work? Can you feel a shift of mindset as you move through your day?
2. How does a fear of failure show up in your work? Why do you try to avoid failure?
3. In what ways can you model a mindset that embraces failure in exchange for innovation and creativity?

4. How can you encourage students, staff, and other school community members to take risks? What holds you back from allowing this?

5. What challenges do you face in your school community when it comes to implementing new ideas or approaches to education?

6. What opportunities do you see for reinventing education in your setting? What is one step you can take today to begin implementing changes?

7. Who can help you promote an innovative mindset? Who can champion failure as a good thing in your school?

8. What failures have taken place in your school that have led to good outcomes?

9. How do you handle rejection? How can your mindset help?

10. Do you encourage high standards, even if it means failing to meet them, or do you feel better when standards are lowered so more can achieve the goal? Consider how each mindset approaches this logic and how it might play out in a school setting.

Mindset: Additional Resources

- **What's My Mindset?:** This assessment determines your current mindset. (http://blog.mindsetworks.com/what-is-my-mindset)

- **What's My Classroom Mindset?:** This assessment measures the mindset in a single classroom environment. (http://blog.mindsetworks.com /what-s-my-classroom-mindset)

- **What's My School Mindset?:** This quiz can identify the growth mindset culture of a school. (http://blog.mindsetworks.com/what-s -my-school-mindset)

- **Maslach Burnout Inventory (MBI) For Educators:** This is a version of the original MBI for use with educators, including teachers, administrators, staff members, and volunteers working in any educational setting. (www.mindgarden.com/316-mbi-educators-survey)

6

How Do My Real-Life Experiences Make Me Unique?

Joe, a middle school principal, was known for getting his hands dirty. When something needed to be fixed, he reached into the various tools stored in his office desk and pulled out the necessary wrench or screwdriver to fix it. One time, when a fire broke out in the school's kitchen, Joe rushed to the scene, broke a fire extinguisher out of its sealed case, and put the fire out before the fire engine had time to leave the station. He was also known for all the "extra" things he did around the school: planting flowers near the front entrance around graduation time, repainting a wall that had been damaged by water, cleaning up messes left by students with upset stomachs. When someone asked him why he was always working so hard, Joe responded, "Sir, I grew up on a dairy farm. There was no vacation, and hard work never stopped. We were up at 5 a.m. and went to bed exhausted at 10 p.m. That's just who I am."

Each of us has a tapestry of life experiences that contribute to who we are and why we are the way we are. For Joe, experiences growing up on a dairy farm created a work ethic and set of expectations he carried into his life as a school leader. In many ways, your formative experiences are as important as the knowledge you gained in school and the formal titles you have earned in your work.

Business advisor, coach, and speaker John Sadowsky (2020) has written about the "value of processing your life's experiences." He convinces leaders to reevaluate their life experiences; as he explains, if they "have something remarkable, it lies not in the particular incidents of [their] life, but rather in [their] ability to look backward, to reflect on the past, and to learn from it" (para. 1). Often, understanding the importance of how to use your real-life experiences is more important than the actual experiences themselves. Sadowsky teaches leaders to understand the following key points about real-life experiences:

- People who use their stories to inspire others generally have no extraordinary life circumstance. They tend to think of their life as typical and usual—which means they have a way of bringing the mundane to life.
- These same people are learned storytellers. That is, they cannot just magically create an inspirational story out of their otherwise typical life. They learn, along the way, to tell stories that can inspire based on everyday events.
- Last, everyone has a useable past—some just learn how to use it better than others to inspire and motivate. (Sadowsky, 2020, paras. 1–3)

Many of us first learn about responsibility, accountability, and work ethic in our first jobs—whether that means watching over siblings or mowing the neighbor's lawn. Everyone's experiences are different, but through purposeful reflection, we can start sorting through our memories and identify where our leadership habits and traits originate. What we learn on the job, in school, and through the stories of others creates a legacy on which our leadership is built. Our past experiences can also serve to foster trust among others. For some parents and community members, knowing that you worked your way from waitress to principal or mechanic to superintendent is humanizing.

Think about how you can incorporate into your PLP the lessons from your first jobs, the first leaders you knew in life, and the lessons you learned early on. Recognize that the ladder of roles you have had in life has built you into a leader today. If you can adequately tell the story of those experiences, then others will start to see you outside of your formal title and better appreciate the qualities that make you an effective school leader.

According to Courtney Calinog (2013), leaders who can learn from and retell lessons from their own life experiences are employing an especially authentic form of leadership. She writes that "one strategy for developing authenticity in leaders is the construction and/or sharing of their life story, providing followers with insight into their authenticity" (para. 1). Results of an online survey Calinog administered found that when leaders learn to tell stories about themselves (even ones that highlight failure, missed opportunities, or regret), their followers see them as more "human, relatable, fallible, or vulnerable" (para. 19), resulting in feelings of greater commitment, engagement, and job satisfaction. "Leaders who want to increase their effectiveness," writes Calinog, "as well as the effectiveness of their followers, by leading authentically from their core values, beliefs, and principles, could benefit greatly from a life stories–oriented leadership development approach" (para. 28).

The Importance of Early Work Experiences

In developing your PLP, we ask that you think critically about your first formal work experience in life. Most people worked part-time at their first jobs as teens, often to save for college, help with family expenses, or pay for extras like a car or clothes. Teens are hired because they are cheap labor and will do jobs that many older workers will not, so first jobs are usually unglamorous and low-paying. Where their value lies is in teaching us our first lessons about professional leadership. For most teens and young adults, first jobs constitute a step outside the home, into the workforce, and directly into a hierarchy of titles and positions. These jobs represent the first time young people relate to a boss or manager, understand the dynamics of customer service, and associate time spent with money earned. They are where we all begin to formulate our perceptions about how a "leader" behaves, acts, and makes decisions.

Consider the following statements from school leaders (and others), reflecting on their first jobs:

- Valerie, a school principal, recalled her first job selling popcorn at a movie theater concession stand. She learned how to pay careful attention when people were talking in that job—a skill that serves her well now in daily conversations with parents and students.

- Elijah, an instructional coach, worked at a large retail clothing store for his first job. He noted that he quickly learned the adage "the customer is always right" and also observed that, as a whole, many people are rude to service workers. He attributes his patience with the teachers he coaches to lessons learned as a cashier at this store. Some of the conversations can be really uncomfortable," he said, "but if I come in with that 'customer's always right' mindset, I can acknowledge their concerns and fear and also build on what is going well in their classroom."

- Imaginix Games founder Anthony Redoblado recalled that his first job at McDonald's as a teenager led him to learn that working harder gets you noticed. "One of the lessons I learned at McDonalds was: the harder I worked, the luckier I got," he said (LAMA, 2018, para. 16). He went on to state that his work ethic today, 20 years later, links back to his days at McDonald's where showing up and working hard was rewarded.

- In an interview with Forbes.com, an equity analyst reported learning in her first job as a stock analyst that attitude and work ethic were at least as important as performance, leading her to seek out companies where she could be her authentic self.

- PBS asked readers of its online newsletter to submit lessons they learned from their first jobs. These lessons included "no job is too menial" from a 57-year-old Wisconsin man who cleaned the floors at his school for his first job. "It taught me not to be ashamed of any kind of work," he wrote. (Kaufman Hogan, 2014, para. 17). Another reader, Vicki Gehlert, worked her first job mucking horse stalls in exchange for riding time. She reflected on what she learned and how it applies to her life decades later. Despite the dirty work, she loved "the camaraderie of similar minds, the smell of the barn, (and) doing something tangible. Forty-four years later, I have shoveled manure in all sorts of jobs, just not the literal kind" (para. 25). She advises that every job has its manure (not literal, but complexities and challenges), but it is all what you make of it.

Consider This

Think about your first job and answer the following prompts.

1. *What was your first job (the first time you earned a formal paycheck)?*

_____

_____

_____

2. *What responsibilities or tasks did you have at your first job?*

_____

_____

_____

3. *What did you enjoy about your first job?*

_____

_____

_____

4. *What did you dislike about your first job?*

_____

_____

_____

5. *What do you think you learned from your first job?*

_____

_____

_____

6. *What do you wish you would have learned from your first job that you did not?*

_____

_____

_____

7. *How do you perceive others who might be starting out their careers or working in low-wage jobs, such as service workers? What advice would you give them, knowing what you know now about the nature of work?*

_____

_____

_____

Our Stories

We would like to share with you some of our own stories to illustrate just how much our early jobs can establish our perceptions of leaders and leadership. First up is Vicki.

Vicki's Story

As a teenager, my first job was as a server at Denny's, where I learned very quickly that there were different types of managers. Some of them I respected and looked forward to working with; others, not so much.

Edward, the general manager, was really a hands-off type of guy. He often sat in his office making schedules, managing payroll, and dealing with supply orders. His rare venture outside the office was never social. He had a low tolerance for goofing off and would often brush past his employees without even saying, "Get out of my way" (let alone "Good morning"). He was the type of manager you respected because he was the boss—not because he'd earned it.

Another manager, Kathy, was also the longest-serving employee on staff, having worked her way up to the position. She had spent most of her adult life as a server and knew the ins and outs of running a successful shift. Kathy was kind and friendly. She was a mentor to the servers, taking us under her wing and generally caring about our success. She got to know us on a personal level, asking me about school, my cross-country team, and my grades. She would answer our questions about restaurant policies and procedures without making us feel inadequate and helped us navigate the intricacies of the ever-changing menu.

Kathy was the type of leader who would stand up to a belligerent customer and remember your birthday. When I went off to college, Kathy sent me notes, stickers, and trinkets to encourage my studies and to let me know she was thinking about me. To Kathy, I was more than a coworker; we were friends, and she took pride in watching me grow up on the job.

Bridget, another manager, seemed physically connected to her clipboard. She stood near the kitchen's swinging door and checked our plates to make sure the twig of parsley was positioned just right on the plates and the flatware we rolled in napkins was free from dishwasher spots. She was quick to correct you if you made an error and was constantly pushing for a quicker turnover of tables. If we could serve faster, we could clear tables faster, which meant we could serve more people. Although Bridget was focused on the details of our work, she was also respectful, task-driven, and precise. She never yelled, sometimes she rewarded us with free dessert when we met our sales goals, and she was generally understanding and supportive when a customer got upset.

My experience working at Denny's gave me a broad view of leadership at a young age. I learned that no two leaders were alike and that different leaders really do have different purposes. Edward had to account for the financial stability of the restaurant, so that job consumed him, as it should. Kathy had a wealth of experience that allowed me to learn from her, and Bridget taught me that being demanding isn't always a bad thing.

Denny's helped me realize as a teenager that to make an enterprise work, everyone must be a piece of the puzzle. While Edward was back in the office managing the paperwork, the other managers helped manage the day-to-day operations. In my faculty role, I see the same concept at work. Without administration and support staff, the faculty would not be able to provide a great learning experience for students.

As a server, I quickly learned the importance of teamwork. I relied on the busboys to help clear the customer's empty plates, on the dishwashers to ensure the coffee mugs and flatware were clean, and on the cooks to prepare the food correctly and in a timely manner. I learned I was only a small piece of the customer experience. As faculty member, I am also part of a team—one that strives to make the student experience amazing. I rely on the university administration to create rules and guidelines to ensure the safety and well-being of our students, the academic coaches to help students create a personalized plan of study, and fellow faculty for support and guidance in the ever-changing landscape of higher education.

As a server, I learned that sometimes things don't go as planned. For instance, when the kitchen printer runs out of paper and nobody realizes it until you ask where the food is for table 10 and the cook stares at you like you're speaking a foreign language. In these types of situations, I had to quickly come up with a plan to ensure the customer remained happy. A solution might have been to alert a manager about the issue, offer an appetizer while the food was being prepared, or provide a free dessert. As a faculty member, when things don't go as planned, I automatically start considering contingency plans without panicking. Learning to roll with the punches has served me well more times than I could ever count.

Gretchen's Story

My first working experiences actually consisted of two jobs: at an old-fashioned shoe store by day and as a Little League umpire at night. Each job taught me something different. At the shoe store, I worked with employees who had made selling shoes a full-time career, meaning they had either inherited the family business or worked their entire adult lives in retail. Other than a couple college-aged kids, the rest of the regular crew were over 50, if not in their 60s or 70s.

Although it felt great to be the young, hip one in the store, I think the most fundamental lesson I learned working there is the importance of respecting those who have lived longer than we have. My coworkers taught me lessons about courtesy, responsibility, and simply caring for people in their old age. I learned how to put shoes on the feet of old ladies with bunions, and every Christmas season I courtesy wrapped hundreds of gift boxes for customers. I did not know it at the time, but I was gaining patience and an appreciation for the experiences of others.

Today, as I write this book in my 40s, most of my coworkers from that job have died. That's a sad thing for me to think about now, but we stayed in touch after I left the job, and when I needed advice or just wanted to feel a piece of home, those were the friends I called. In my job now, where faculty I work with can be in the later decades of life, these skills are still much in use. I now work with multiple generations of colleagues, so I am constantly navigating communication preferences and work styles. I serve students, who, much like customers, deserve to be listened to and valued. However, as with every job, there is a fair share of paperwork, email, and mundane tasks that need to be addressed in order to get through a day.

The umpire job was a bit more controversial. As you may imagine, with Little League players come parents, coaches, and fans who can be obnoxious, vile, and annoying. In that job, I learned to stand firm. I was not perfect by any means, and no decision I made as an umpire changed anyone's life, but the job taught me how to make quick decisions and stand by them. I got used to hearing the opinions of others and quickly became aware of how much a "good game, Ump" coming from a passerby meant after a game. The job also gave me the ability to let things go and move on after a decision without dwelling on it for days or weeks.

As a college professor today, there are times when decisions must be made quickly and decisively. I can do this, for the most part, without hearing the voice of an inner critic, largely thanks to those formative experiences. In addition, this job gave me a wild appreciation for coaches, umpires, and athletes who pour their hearts into what they love. This resonates with me as an author, since writing is my sport. Finally, I think watching so much baseball helped me see that finding something you love can bring a great sense of satisfaction to one's life.

Your Story

Think about your first job again and answer the following questions in the spaces provided.

1. *Who was the "leader" at your first job? Describe him or her.*

_____

_____

_____

_____

2. *What did you learn at your first job?*

_____

_____

_____

_____

3. *What lessons from that first job are still with you today?*

_____

_____

_____

_____

4. *What parts of your role as a school leader remind you of your first job? Why?*

_____

_____

_____

The Impact of Schooling

Teacher and school leader Cynthia "Mama J" Johnson often talks about the impact her own teachers had on her future career as an educator. As a child growing up in Missouri, Johnson experienced the reality of economic stress and unclear expectations. She recalls the influence of one teacher during her middle school years in a news article:

> I had one teacher that looked at me and didn't worry about all the things that were going on in my life: that I was a child of poverty, that I stuttered, that I was in special classes, that I couldn't read very well. He wasn't worried about that. He involved me in speech and drama and . . . took me to competitions, and in that first competition, I won first place. (Salisbury, 2019, para. 11)

Johnson credits Mr. Bell, her 8th grade speech and drama teacher, with changing her life's trajectory. Johnson's career has included roles as a classroom teacher, school leader, speaker, and national consultant. What we love about her story is not only that she managed such achievements because one teacher believed in her but also that she applies those lessons to her professional practice today. Here's what she told *Education Week* in 2018:

> The lesson I learned that still influences my teaching today is forming relationships with students and connecting them to activities in the school that can save their lives. This lesson has been the focus

of my educational career for the past 30 years. I always remember how Mr. Bell made me feel and that he believed in my ability until I had this belief in myself. I, in turn, have used the same philosophy since I started my teaching journey in 1987. As a forensic and special education teacher, my students gave me the nickname "Mama J" because of the powerful teacher-student relationships formed. (Ferlazzo, 2018)

Of course, not all of us had educational experiences as positive as Mama J's. In talking with school leaders for this book, we were struck by the principals and teachers who said they entered the field of education *in spite* of the teachers they'd had. One teacher, Stephanie, recalled a teacher telling her that she would never be good at math, so she might as well not take the advanced placement courses she was well-qualified to take. Stephanie spent years making up for lost time in her own preparation to become a high school math teacher. She shared with us that the one thing she wants all her students to know is that she believes in them no matter what. Not a single teacher had believed in her, and she doesn't want any student to ever feel the way she did.

Our experiences as students can also dictate how familiar we are with situations we encounter as school leaders. For example, leaders who attended high-poverty urban schools may have faced institutional racism, a lack of discipline, or inexperienced teachers and administrators—and thus have some idea of ways to navigate these challenges.

Take Chloe, for example. A middle school principal in an urban school, Chloe grew up attending a school much like the one in which she works. She grew up on public assistance, ate her one hot meal of the day at school, and graduated in a dress handed down from her three older sisters. When she sees her students, she sees a bit of herself in them. She recognizes that some of them go home to an empty house like she did when she was young and that some of them long for the consistency of the school day. These experiences have made her a staunch advocate for making resources such as take-home meals and free school supplies available to students.

Perhaps you work in the school you once attended or, alternatively, lead a school much different than the ones in which you grew up in. Either way, your days as a student walk alongside you in the school hallways today. What experiences are you still carrying?

Consider This

Looking back, how would you describe the school(s) you attended?

_____

_____

_____

_____

_____

What sticks out in your mind?

_____

_____

_____

_____

_____

How were the schools you attended growing up different than the one in which you work today?

_____

_____

_____

_____

_____

What teacher do you remember the most? Why?

_____

_____

_____

_____

_____

What part of your own schooling motivated you to go into education? (This might be a positive or negative experience.)

_____

_____

_____

_____

_____

The Impact of Our Personal History

Outside of work and school, think of the other influences that have seeped into your adult life: how your parents or caretakers raised you, the types of homes in which you lived, the relationships you maintained with family and friends. Our upbringings influence our professional lives in the form of the values, beliefs, and principles we picked up along the way.

According to psychologist James L. Creighton (2019), we tend to frame our own life stories in three ways: as family myths, as descriptions of the kind of person we are, or through the lens of a traumatic event (like the death of a parent or having been abused). Creighton argues that we should, instead, "restory" our lives by thinking about past experiences as "chapters" in our story and compare our reactions today to the events in our past that may have formed how we think, feel, or respond. For example, a conflict you face today related to changing jobs might be influenced by the frequent moving you experienced as the child of a military parent, with your responses to the situation dictated by beliefs you formed as a child facing the same issues. If we can somehow relate our own lived experiences to the decisions we make today, we can better understand the wholeness of our being.

Our Ongoing Personal Histories

As important as early life experiences are to us, so too are the challenges we face today, in the middle of our daily lives. If we are fighting with a spouse or struggling with a physical ailment, these issues also influence how and why we make the decisions we do. One school principal, Patty, shared with us how her diagnosis of multiple sclerosis changed her outlook on mentoring teachers. She noted that she began to ask teachers to focus on their own well-being first rather than on the increasing demands of the job, knowing that the only way one could survive in education was to be physically and mentally well.

Conclusion

Working a variety of jobs during our lifetimes increases our exposure to different leadership styles and types, both good and bad. Depending on the job, situation, and location, you may have learned from some exceptional leaders in your first job or endured the lessons of a toxic leader. Ultimately, though, both kinds of experiences helped form who you are today and offer opportunities for reflection.

Consider This

Charlie, now an assistant superintendent for an urban district, shared his first-job experiences as a cashier at a grocery store. He specifically recalled this job as one of the worst learning experiences of his life. The manager, he recalled, verbally harassed the staff, threw produce against the wall when it wasn't arranged perfectly, and occasionally dipped into the cashier's drawer to pull money for his personal use.

"He was just a horrible example to all of us who were watching how adults behave in the world," Charlie remembered. "It was so much more than his yelling and erratic behavior—he just did not know how to lead, and his frustrations caused all of us to not want to follow him because of how poorly he treated us. As a leader now, I am really cautious of what I am doing when others watch, and I strive to project a sense of calm because I know what it's like to be around an unpredictable leader—and I hate it!"

Whether we know it or not, past leaders have left their legacies with us. In our formative professional experiences, we observed how leaders treated people, made decisions, navigated ethical dilemmas, and generally moved through life. We want to not only remember (and replicate) the great leaders who taught us so well but also avoid repeating the mistakes of leaders who were toxic or ineffective.

Reflection Questions

1. What do you wish your school community knew about your background that they do not know now? Why is this important to you?

2. What skills or attributes do you have that prepared you for your job today? Where did you learn those skills?

3. What would people from your early or first jobs say about your work ethic? How has it changed over time?

4. How could sharing your early work experiences (or past jobs) lead to better connections between colleagues?

5. What lessons do you carry with you from teachers or leaders at the schools you attended?

6. Talk with some colleagues at work about their first jobs. What did you learn that you did not know before you conversed?

7. What influence does your personal life have on your decision making in school today? How can you know when your personal history might be guiding you rather than critical thinking?

8. How much time do you spend getting to hear about other community members' personal histories? Do you think you should spend more time doing this? Why or why not?

9. What does your school community assume about your background that simply is not accurate? How can you change this?

10. Why is it important to reflect on your background as you create your PLP?

Additional Resource: Real-Life Experiences

- **DISC Personality Test:** This assessment helps you understand your personality at work, which can help you describe past work experiences. (www.truity.com/test/disc-personality-test)

7

Crafting My PLP

Brady began his first principalship at the middle school where he had taught music and coached football for 12 years. The previous principal recently retired, and Brady was set on forging a new path for a school that had been steeped in tradition and outdated instructional practices for too many years. Brady had heard the complaints of his colleagues and had even been one of the harshest critics of the prior administration himself, so he felt the weight of expectations on his shoulders as he began his new job. Brady knew his role was to be a change agent. Teachers needed access to updated technology, new curricula, and a new behavior-management model. He was ready for the challenge but unsure how to convince the teachers he had worked alongside for more than a decade that the hard work of change was worth it.

Brady struggled to identify his priorities. He sought input from his trusted mentors and listened to suggestions from parents and students, but he still felt lost. Somehow, he knew he had to define his leadership so the school community understood his vision. Part of leadership, he began to realize, is embracing who you are and what brought you to this moment in time—not the opinions of others, what outsiders want you to be, or who you wished you could emulate. Brady started to develop his own personal leadership philosophy, and in doing so, gained confidence in his skills. The words weren't perfect, but they were there, and they guided his thinking. This process of putting words to paper, Brady realized, provided him with a sense of purpose and direction as a principal.

The assessments and reflection questions with which you engaged in earlier chapters were preparation to craft your personal leadership philosophy. This chapter will guide you, step by step, through the writing process, putting the results of those assessments and reflective questions to use.

We created a four-step framework to guide you as you develop your first draft. Please be aware that this will not be a quick process; you will not complete your PLP in a single writing session. Forming your leadership philosophy through writing will take time and commitment. It will likely take several drafts as well as input from coworkers, friends, and family. Don't be afraid to make mistakes, discard drafts, or simply start over. Remember, the process of creating a PLP is meant to stimulate personal reflection and professional growth and to help you comprehensively examine your actions as a leader. In fact, the reflection process necessary to create a PLP is just as important as the end product, given the amount of self-awareness it takes to formulate a comprehensive PLP statement.

It is also important to recognize that just because you have never created a written statement about the way you lead does not mean you don't have an existing leadership philosophy. If you have ever managed a group of people, then you probably have one (Coppola, 2002). This chapter will guide you in making that leadership philosophy clear, not only to others but also to yourself.

The PLP framework is intended both to support the creative writing process and to help ensure that you include the various components discussed so far in this book. Each section of this chapter will guide you back to the chapter where you took notes, jotted down ideas, and completed assessments. Additionally, space will be provided for you to begin brainstorming the information you want to include in your final PLP. Use this space to write down whatever comes to mind, then later—once all your ideas are written down—you can decide what to retain in your finished product.

Part 1: Introduction and Leadership Style

The first component of your PLP is an introduction of yourself as a leader. Look back at the reflection questions in Chapter 1 and consider who you are as a leader—as well as any assumptions you want to correct. Remember that your official title only tells a small part of your story. In a sense, you hold two identities: one based on your leadership style, lived experiences, mindset, and core values; and another made of others' perceptions of you.

The description of who you are as a leader should flow nicely into an explanation of your leadership style. Share your style through an example, description, or explanation—don't just say you are a directing, guiding, or enabling leader, since most people will not understand what these terms mean. Instead, use your own words to describe the results of the leadership style assessment earlier in this book. Bring these results to life through an example or illustration connected to your work. Another approach is to explain how you have put each leadership style into action or to rephrase your responses to the reflection questions at the end of Chapter 3.

Here are some additional writing prompts to help get the brainstorming process started:

- What do you hope those you lead will appreciate about your leadership style?
- How would you describe the relationship between you and those you lead?

- How would you explain the respective responsibilities of leaders and those they lead?
- How are these relationships and responsibilities reflected in your leadership methods?
- How are your leadership methods attentive to the diverse expectations and needs of those you lead?
- How do your personal characteristics and leadership style relate to your leadership behaviors?

Part 1 Brainstorming Space

_____

_____

_____

_____

_____

_____

_____

_____

_____

_____

Part 2: Core Values

As discussed in Chapter 4, core values are beliefs and principles we generally consider to be nonnegotiable and tend to remain consistent over time. They are at the heart of who we are and how we behave. Review the core values assessment you completed in Chapter 4, then describe your core values and how they influence your leadership approach. Consider the following prompts as you brainstorm:

- What is most important to you in the workplace? Why?
- What events, people, things, or processes have shaped you, regardless of your educational and professional background?
- What professional accomplishment are you most proud of?
- Describe a time you were happiest and most productive at work. What responsibilities did you have?
- Have you ever had to juggle more projects than you had time for? If so, how did you prioritize?
- Describe your ideal team. Have you ever worked with a team that embodied these characteristics? If so, share your experience.

Part 2 Brainstorming Space

_____

_____

_____

_____

_____

_____

_____

_____

_____

_____

_____

_____

_____

_____

_____

_____

_____

_____

_____

_____

_____

_____

_____

_____

Part 3: Mindset

Your mindset is the way you approach problem solving, success and failure, and opportunities for learning. It can waver between growth-oriented or fixed. Whereas a growth mindset is open to innovation, change, and learning from failure, a fixed mindset favors the status quo, aims for consistency, and limits exposure to failure. Your mindset can affect how you are perceived by those you lead. Consider the mindset activity you completed in Chapter 5. What emoji did you circle the most in Figure 5.1 (p. 71)? At what points during the day does your mindset tend to be more fixed or more growth-oriented? Review the reflection questions at the end of Chapter 5 and summarize your responses, using a specific example of how your mindset influences your leadership. Here are some writing prompts to consider when brainstorming about your mindset:

- What mindset do you want your followers to embrace? What about your students? Teachers? Why?
- At what times, if any, does a fixed mindset serve your school setting well? What about a growth-oriented mindset?
- How would those who watch you lead identify your mindset?
- Describe an example of a tough or critical piece of feedback you received. What was it and what did you do about it?
- What is your view on continuous learning?
- What helps you bounce back when things are not moving in the direction you hoped for?

Part 3 Brainstorming Space

_____

_____

_____

_____

_____

_____

_____

_____

_____

_____

_____

_____

_____

_____

_____

_____

_____

_____

_____

_____

_____

Part 4: Real-life Experiences

The last part of the PLP asks you to share your real-life experiences and how they influence the decisions you make as a school leader today. These experiences are a compilation of your work history, your educational history, and your personal history. Real-life experiences provide insight into your motivations, your beliefs about work and leadership, and how you view your role as a leader within a school. Review the reflective questions you answered in Chapter 6. Here are some additional prompts to consider:

- How will you continue growing as a leader?
- How have your real-life experiences changed the way you approach leadership over time?
- How will you use real-life experiences to improve your leadership?
- What professional experiences do you have that can add value to your school community?
- What skills do you consider to be your greatest strengths?
- What skills do you consider to be your biggest weaknesses?

Part 4 Brainstorming Space

_____

_____

_____

_____

_____

_____

_____

_____

_____

_____

_____

_____

_____

_____

_____

_____

_____

_____

_____

_____

_____

_____

_____

_____

_____

_____

Tips to Get Started with Your First PLP Draft

- As you begin to think about solidifying the first few sentences of your PLP, it can be difficult to overcome the desire to have it be perfect the first time. The PLP does not work that way, however. It's a bit like perfecting your favorite recipe. The first time you make it, it turns out just fine; the second time, you add more flavor and it's even better; then, each subsequent time you make it, the end result becomes better and better.

- Before you start writing, know your audience. Having a clear picture of who your audience is will allow you to set the tone as you begin to write. Your audience might include students, community members, colleagues, future employers, even people outside the educational field. As you consider your audience, be sure to also do your research. If you are creating the PLP specifically to apply for a new position, you may want to modify the tone or approach to align with the hiring institution.

- Use a narrative, first-person approach. This voice will allow the PLP to be both personal and reflective (Chism, 1998; Coppola, 2002).

- The PLP should be a maximum of one page long. We recommend you double space and use a 12-point font for ease of reading.

- Don't just repeat what is on your résumé. The purpose of your PLP is to highlight your leadership style, lived experiences, mindset, and core values—not to offer a rundown of the positions you've held.

- Use the brainstorming spaces in this chapter to craft one or two sentences for each PLP section. Then start elaborating on each of those sentences, providing concrete ideas and examples.

- Another way of interweaving the content from the previous chapters together is to read through your notes and highlight ideas or observations that have come up more than once. Think of these as "themes" that might help you structure your PLP.

- Start with a "hook." Your readers will be most engaged when they read your opening line. Some strategies to hook your reader include beginning with a question, a quote, or even an event from your past that can set the tone for your PLP.

- Be sincere and unique. Avoid clichés, especially ones about how much passion you have for education, leading, or being part of a school community. Make sure your PLP demonstrates that you care about the content you are sharing within it.

- Make your points specific rather than abstract. General statements can be interpreted in many ways, so make sure to support statements with specific examples (Grundman, 2006.) Here are some tips from Kearns and Sullivan (2011):

  - Reflect on a leadership experience when you were effective. Write about that "great moment" by sharing how it exemplified your leadership style.

  - Share a "not-so-great moment" when you were not satisfied with how a leadership decision played out. How do both the "great moment" and "not-so-great-moment" exemplify what you value about your leadership style?

  - At the beginning of the PLP, provide a story that describes a fundamental moment in your leadership journey. The rest of your PLP should incorporate descriptions of how your leadership style, core values, or mindset were influenced by that event.

  - Introduce a metaphor at the beginning of your PLP. The rest of your philosophy should incorporate descriptions of specific leadership moments that connect to the metaphor.

- Avoid jargon and technical terms, as they can be off-putting to some readers (Browne, 2017). Make sure your PLP contains content that can be broadly understood (Chism, 1998).

- It's OK to write more content than you need. Your draft might be several pages longer than the completed PLP if you thoroughly complete the framework.
- Dust off assessments, surveys, and workshop activities you have completed over the years. Review the results, identifying themes about your personality, how you collaborate, your strengths, and your work habits. This information can help you clarify your leadership style, core values, and mindset.

Committing to Your First Draft

Now it's time to dive into writing the first draft of your PLP. The key to this is to write freely. Don't fret over word choice or imperfections; just get some ideas on paper. You can come back to wordsmith things later. Right now, forget about who will read this or what they will think of you when they do. For this moment, just write.

As you begin to write your draft, if you find yourself getting stuck on a certain section, it's fine to skip ahead. You can always come back later, and sometimes focusing on a different section of the PLP will give you fresh insight that can help you successfully push through your creative block. Consider the blank paper a canvas, and remember that there is no wrong or right way to craft the beautiful portrait of yourself you are about to create.

Allow for imperfections in your first draft. If something feels awkward, just write it down and come back to it later. If you are stuck for words, leave a space and return to it at another time. It is important to realize that your first draft will not be your final draft. Turn off your internal critic as you write. If you rewrite the same paragraph over and over, trying to make it as perfect as possible, you'll never finish. As you create your first draft, you'll likely notice typos and poor word choices. At this stage of the writing process, these errors are not a bad thing. You will have plenty of time to clean up your PLP during the editing process.

Most importantly, do not delete or scratch out any content you don't like. Instead, just keep writing. The words and phrases you generate during this drafting process may prove useful down the road. Don't make any permanent removals for now. You may see something of value in your first draft later as you revise and edit. Resist the urge to stop and edit as you're writing your PLP. Leave a blank space if you can't think of a word, a quote, or a piece of information. Put a squiggle under words you're not sure you spelled right. Check and clarify details after you get all your thoughts down on paper.

Avoiding Common Missteps

Writing a PLP is not a one-time event. It requires time, reflection, revision, and realization. Before moving forward, we want to take some time to walk you through other drafts and show you how they evolved through revision.

Our experiences walking many school leaders through this process have allowed us to find common patterns that leaders tend to fall into—as well as emerging patterns around different types of philosophies. We have categorized these into larger types and offered some insights on why these particular angles of PLP writing can be problematic in telling your leadership story effectively. What we hope to illustrate by sharing these outtakes from different "types" of writing is that some of the challenges and pitfalls of writing a PLP really arise when you (the author) struggle with authenticity and honesty about who you are. Now is the time to embrace your talents—not hide behind a mess of jargon and ideologies trying to pretend to be what others expect or want of you. As you'll see, the more you own your unique voice, the more powerful and clear your PLP will be.

The Dreamer

Dreamers tend to have an optimistic view of their personal leadership philosophy but provide little evidence to support this. Dreamers are afraid to be vulnerable in writing and rely on maxims and broad philosophical statements to build their philosophy. Here's a portion of a dreamer's PLP:

> Children are the future. I am a leader who believes that success begins with collaborating, setting goals, and then working together to achieve those goals. I will embrace failure in order to encourage creativity. We will see failures as learning opportunities, while also examining our successes as opportunities to grow. We can all learn!

Consider adding evidence of real-life experiences from the beginning. Instead of saying "children are the future," start with something you've witnessed or experienced that demonstrates how children possess hope and promise in real life. Then share an example of your leadership style in action—something you did or said as a leader that really shows how you lead and how your leadership builds on the hope you find in children today. Be sure to include evidence for all four key components of the PLP. With all the pieces in place, you'll be able to complete a comprehensive leadership profile.

The Overconfident Leader

Overconfident leaders inspire teachers to innovate and feel secure in their school. As Victor Lipman (2017) notes, "People don't want to follow leaders who show uncertainty and anxiety. Fear is contagious. As is confidence, but in a more productive direction" (para. 6). However, a personal leadership philosophy that exudes too much confidence may be read as boastful, insincere, or self-centered. Here's a sample from an overconfident leader's PLP:

> I am a genuine and driven leader who strives for excellence in everything I do. I try to help those I come into contact with understand there is no singular way to learn, teach, or serve. I hope to take the gifts my coworkers bring to the table and mesh those strengths with the mission of my school.

Instead of this, we suggest finding a happy medium between confident and humble. You will go on to explain how real-life experiences have built your confidence so it is perceived as more authentic. You should also provide examples of collaboration to illustrate what you're looking for.

The Generalist

Without specific examples, it can be really hard to conceptualize what this leader is like in real life—this is what we consider a generalist, or someone who really doesn't take a position on anything. It's great that the leader uses accessible language, but we also need a clear indication of style and real-life experiences. Examine this example from a generalist's PLP:

> Listening to students, parents, and teachers will guide my decisions. I will walk beside my colleagues, not in front of them. I hope students and staff see me as approachable and willing to take responsibility for my actions while holding others to that same standard.

Think about adding a statement about leadership style and integrating it with the statements about collaboration and working alongside followers. Listening is an important leadership skill, but why? How has it affected your relationships specifically?

The Spiritualist

Humility is a positive trait in leadership. It shows a willingness to learn, listen to others, and admit one's mistakes. This following builds trust and invites followers to buy into the leader's aspirations, but it lacks a clear example of how the leader uses these skills in the school. What does it mean to be a "transformational leader" in this philosophy? How can your story be told in a way that embraces your passion yet does not appear inauthentic?

> I am called to be a teacher. My entire life has prepared me to be who I am today. I seek to provide justice, peace, and inspiration to

my school community. I am a transformational leader who seeks to accompany others toward a meaningful professional life that brings out the very best in our students and teachers.

It can be helpful to integrate a school's mission or vision within your PLP, including specific examples of how your decisions have supported that mission. Additionally, it might be helpful to explain terms such as *transformational leader* to an outsider or what it means to be "called" to be a teacher, perhaps with examples showing this in your professional practice.

The Risk-Taker

Leaders who are willing to take risks are often seen as innovators and creators; that's a growth mindset, after all. Without risks, organizations stay static and often fall behind in current trends. Risk-averse leaders also tend to foster fear and distrust. This leader's philosophy embraces growth, change, and trust. However, risk-takers also can appear precarious in their decision making, maybe acting irrationally or without first carefully thinking through the consequences of their actions.

> I am a charismatic leader who likes the adventure of leadership. In my job as principal, I want teachers to experiment with teaching and know that failure is acceptable. I encourage staff to solve problems by considering innovative solutions, such as last year when our elementary teachers facilitated parent-teacher conferences virtually to enable more connection with parents who couldn't attend meetings in person. I also know that everything does not go as planned, but I'd rather take the risk than wonder what could have been—which is how I ended up in school leadership. I empower others by showing trust and belief in their accomplishments.

To alleviate concerns about risk-taking and to invoke trust, this leader could further explain how risk-taking without success (otherwise known as failure) is supported. Additionally, it might help to add an example of a time risk-taking caused a negative reaction or was perceived imperfectly by the school community and how this leader overcame that reaction in order to produce results.

The Changer

We love a school leader who wants to cause disruption and improvement within a struggling system. This personal leadership philosophy embraces the idea that the leader, as one person, can begin the ripple effect that causes larger change.

> I began teaching in order to change the cultural dynamics in the community where I grew up. My elementary school had almost no resources—we used to kick around old soda cans at recess and were lucky if our class actually had a full set of matching textbooks from the same decade. I became a school leader not just to respond to conditions but to lead the charge to change how we provide for our students, both physically and emotionally. My work is focused on changing one life at a time.

This PLP succeeds at illustrating a picture of the school leader's history—and why that history is still important today. What can strengthen this further by diving into the story of why the leader sees the school of the past as something to leave behind, rather than replicate? What specifically does it mean to be an "instigator of change"?

The List-Maker

Lists can be direct and easy to read, and they offer a way to rank issues according to importance. However, lists can also leave room for interpretation. Without any explanation or illustrations, it can be difficult to conceptualize what the leader means by each descriptor. Read this PLP, which began in list form:

> My goal as a leader is to be:
> - accountable
> - accessible

- friendly
- open-minded

Things I will not be:
- bossy
- invasive
- disrespectful

> Staff in my school know I always have an open door and will work with them through any problem they face.

Lists are great for brainstorming since they allow us to capture our ideas quickly without having to take much time to explain. However, a PLP should include more context, so this leader should finesse each item to include information explaining why it is important and how it applies within the school setting.

The Humble Leader

Humble leaders are generally very likeable because they show a willingness to accept imperfections. When we work with humble leaders, we notice their keen ability to listen and serve others. However, the desire to be a humble leader can be hard to explain in a PLP. This example does a nice job of providing examples of times the leader has acted humbly. Be careful, though, not to oversell yourself—it is impossible to be humble in all the roles you fill in life, so try to focus in on your role as a school leader.

> My leadership style is adaptive, inclusive, and follows the servant leadership philosophy. I am an authentic leader who employs a transformational approach to guide my leadership style. I enjoy collaborating with individuals and teams who share a common principle of keeping the students at the forefront of our work. I believe in playing to people's strengths in order to set them up for future success; giving credit where credit is due; setting high standards with accountability for myself and others. Failure is a teacher of mine. I am willing to engage in difficult conversations. My faith

and lived experiences as a husband, father, teacher, coach, and life-long learner all inform my decision making.

In this portion of a PLP, the leader presents evidence of humility without needing to come out and say, "I'm humble." What would help strengthen this PLP is an example of some of the more challenging aspects of humility—perhaps an explanation of how failure has taught the leader lessons or an example of the "difficult conversations" he or she has experienced as a school leader.

The Questioner

Asking questions is a familiar way to start a formal speech or prepare a paper. It provides the hook necessary to get the reader immediately involved in what's to come. However, asking questions without ever providing realistic, identifiable answers can leave the reader wondering why the question was even asked in the first place. This philosophy snippet does a great job of hooking the reader, but it continues to ask too many questions without clearly identifying the important pieces of the leader's philosophy.

> What does it mean to be a leader? Where do I want to go in my life and in my leadership role? I aspire to lead a school where I am an integral piece of the educational environment. As a former team leader and experienced district leader, do I always know that I'm making the best decision? Am I willing to make mistakes and learn from the mistakes I make? What do I value? Do I always have a good attitude? Who am I as a leader?

It's acceptable to open your PLP with a question or pose a question within the PLP, but try to limit your use of questions to those you're willing to answer using concrete examples of your leadership.

The Boss

Leading does come with responsibility and accountability, but a philosophy like this can seem like an expression of power or authority. Even though leaders need to be able to take charge and make decisions, a PLP should consider its intended audience. If it minimizes the input of the school community or positions the leader above others, dissatisfaction is likely to follow.

> Leadership is an important role in any school setting. I've basically grown up in this district, from earning my diploma here to teaching high school history. I know the importance of accountability and ensuring that teachers do what they are told to do. One team member can make the entire team fail, and it is my job to prevent that from happening. I make my intentions clear and visit classrooms often so teachers know I am watching. My evaluations are honest and inspire teachers to make changes to better their teaching. I know leadership is my life's calling.

This leader should consider softening the language to be more inclusive and compassionate. Prepare a PLP in a way that builds confidence in your authority. Rather than saying things like you expect teachers to "do what they are told to do," suggest that you support different ways for teachers to do their work.

The Buzzwordsmith

Working in schools, it is easy to get accustomed to using educational jargon and buzzwords familiar within the walls of the school. However, it is important to realize that the PLP is intended not only for those within the school community but also for those who might not be familiar with the buzzwords used in the workplace. The following philosophy uses too many acronyms and jargon.

> Today's school leader must be ready to innovate and prepare students to be college- or career-ready. As a 1:1 school leader, I am proficient in both formative and summative learning assessments and how those tell the story of what teachers do on a daily basis in the classroom. In my time here, I have supported collaborative teaching, PLCs, and implementation of technology for the NGSS.

> I design staff development in a scaffolded manner that allows each
> staff member to analyze his or her own metacognition. I value learn-
> ing, and I know the teachers and students in my school see me live
> this every day.

Try to limit the use of vocabulary or lingo that only educators know. Concepts like 1:1, PLCs, formative assessments, and the NGSS can be clarified by providing a simple definition or explanation within the context of the PLP without distracting the reader from the document's overall flow. Have a friend or family member who works in a field outside education identify when your PLP might head down this path.

The Oversharer

Your personal history can be a great background for your PLP. It is what makes you unique and relatable. Oversharing, though, means you've placed the reader in an uncomfortable place. Discussing personal issues, such as divorce, abuse, or other such extremely intimate matters, should only be done with care and a clear purpose. Consider this example:

> I was raised by a single mom in the outskirts of Denver. My mom,
> who never graduated from high school herself, always made sure
> I put school first in my life, even if it meant she had to work two
> jobs to pay our bills and my college tuition. As a single mom myself,
> having left an abusive relationship, I have seen the difficulty of over-
> coming. After my divorce, I wondered if I would ever find happiness
> again. I did, but in ways I never expected. As I moved from substitute
> teacher to classroom teacher to assistant principal, I always remem-
> bered the sacrifices my mom made and how the parents of many
> of my students were doing the same thing for their own children.
> As a leader, I value honesty and integrity. My role in the school is to
> ensure every student has a chance and that every communication
> we have builds student confidence to finish school, just like I did so
> many years ago.

Even though the personal touch here is a great lead into the larger story, the leader should consider limiting the focus on her personal life, concentrating instead on that initial story of how watching her hard-working mom inspired her to see leadership in a distinctive way. It is possible to demonstrate ambition, dedication, and commitment without sharing details that are highly personal.

Conclusion

Just as every leader's journey is unique, so, too, are the ways each of us capture our experiences and talents in a PLP. The lessons here are simple: write, rewrite, cross out, erase, replace, and rewrite again. Move words around. Find synonyms. Think about what makes you unique. Find your voice. The missteps we share here are not fatal; they are just trends we've seen in the many PLPs we've helped shepherd along in the writing process. Focus on simply getting words on paper at this stage. We'll worry about the rest later in this book.

Taking time to carefully write your PLP is an investment in your personal brand that affects each reader's impression of you as a school leader. If the idea here is to move beyond your title, you must express yourself in a way that makes your stories approachable and your qualities authentic. Avoiding common missteps is part of the writing process, and so, too, is recognizing the individuality of each PLP. This is why there is no strict formula for a successful PLP.

Your philosophy should not be a long, drawn-out liturgy. It should be precise enough to fit within the confines of one page, and you should be able to share it on your school website. It should prepare you fully to respond when asked in your next interview, "So, what's your leadership philosophy?"

Reflection Questions

1. Reread what you've written in the brainstorming spaces of this chapter. Does your writing exhibit any of the drawbacks discussed in the chapter's second half? If so, consider how you might rewrite to be more inclusive and accessible.

2. What would someone who doesn't know you but reads your PLP on your school website learn about you? What is the tone your work sets?

3. What is the most difficult part of your PLP to write? Why?

4. Of the different types of examples shared in this chapter, which do you find hardest to relate to? Why?

5. When you are writing your PLP, who do you envision reading it? Does that affect what you want to write? Why or why not?

6. What do you think is unique about your philosophy?

7. What do you wish you could articulate better in your philosophy?

8. Put yourself in the role of teacher, student, parent, or community member. Read your draft material from their point of view. What questions do you have after considering their perspectives?

PLP Examples

Everly, a middle school instructional coach, found her niche helping teachers become better at their craft. In the six years since leaving her 6th grade classroom, she had successfully coached over 50 new and veteran teachers. Her daily role consisted of visiting classrooms, meeting with teachers, observing student engagement, and collaborating with school leaders on areas that needed improvement in order to foster student learning. Over time, Everly became a strong advocate for small class sizes and manageable workloads for teachers.

She also felt her perception of education change through the years. When she was a classroom teacher, she was idealistic. When she moved into the instructional coach role, she became more task-oriented and driven by student success. As she worked more and more alongside school leaders, she began to understand their challenges and often witnessed just how much work they were doing behind the scenes to make teachers' jobs easier. Her philosophy, it seemed, evolved depending on which role she was serving in and who she was working beside. Was this *a sign of her inconsistency or lack of commitment to one faction over the other, or was it a normal evolution expected as an educator grows and matures into new responsibilities?*

In education, it can be easy to fall into habits that occur school year after school year without recognizing the magnitude of your personal growth or development. Additionally, what we once held as goals or ideals shift and change over time, leaving us wondering what the next steps in our life might look like. In this chapter, you will read four sample PLPs built around the four essential elements shared in this book: leadership style, core values, mindset, and real-life experiences. For some of them, we've shared both the initial draft and the revised version. Respond to the prompts in the spaces provided after each sample PLP.

Sample PLP #1

Heather is an assistant principal at an arts academy.

Heather's First Draft

As an energetic and passionate school leader, I seek to ensure that all students achieve their maximum potential. Relationships are at the heart of what I treasure: collaborating in a team environment with other educators to support all students. I value and utilize input from all stakeholders, as well as data, to make decisions that contribute to the success of my school. My work experiences as a paraeducator and former classroom teacher taught me to put people first. I grew up in a school like this one, and I want students to dream big. I am zealous in my desire to build a positive school culture where everybody matters; from the custodian to the principal, all staff members play a role in raising student achievement. Special education is the heart of my mission and ensuring that all students can access an appropriate education. For me, leadership is a verb, and I believe that I lead through my actions—working side by side with educators to propel all students forward.

What is Heather's leadership style? How do you know?

_____

_____

_____

What are Heather's core values? How do you know?

_____

_____

_____

What do we know about Heather's mindset? What words or phrases teach us about her mindset?

_____

_____

_____

What real-life experiences did Heather share that made her unique?

_____

_____

_____

What are the strengths of Heather's PLP?

_____

_____

_____

What suggestions would you provide to help Heather improve this PLP?

_____

_____

_____

Our Suggestions to Heather

After we walked Heather through the PLP framework outlined in this book, she completed this second version. Note some of the questions we posed to her within the parentheses.

> For me, leadership is a verb, and I believe that I lead through my actions, working side-by-side with educators to propel all students forward. As an energetic and passionate *(Take out one of these adjectives—energetic or passionate. It's just too much at once.)* school leader, I seek to ensure that all students achieve their maximum

potential. *(How about "in their learning capacity" or something to capture that thought?)* Relationships are at the heart of what I treasure *(What does this really mean? Try to reword it to not be so dreamy. That is, look at the last part of the sentence, which is about collaboration—how does that work together with your interest in relationships?)*—collaborating in a team environment with other educators to support all students. I value and utilize input from all stakeholders *(That's really broad—because ALL means ALL—but what does that really mean for you as a school leader?)* as well as data to make decisions that contribute to the success of my school. *(Do you have an example to support this? Show me how your school is successful.)* My work experiences as a paraeducator and former classroom teacher taught me to put people first. *(What did you learn in these roles?)* I grew up in a school like this one, and I want students to dream big. *(What, exactly, about this school reminds you of what you experienced yourself as a student?)* I am zealous *(How about "I aim to build"?)* to build a positive school culture where everybody matters; from the custodian to the principal, all staff members play a role in raising student achievement. *(We think you can remove these next lines: ~~Special education is the heart of my mission and ensuring that all students can access an appropriate education. For me, leadership is a verb, and I believe that I lead through my actions—working side by side with educators to propel all students forward.~~)*

How would the tone of Heather's philosophy change if she provided the examples and was more specific in the areas we identified for her in our comments?

_____

_____

_____

As an outsider reading this, what do you know about Heather without ever meeting her?

_____

_____

_____

What do you wish you knew more about Heather? What should she add or change to make her PLP more personal?

_____

_____

_____

Sample PLP #2

Genevieve is a team leader at an elementary school.

Genevieve's First Draft

Leadership is a privilege. My daily work with students allows me to get to know them, grow with them, and learn alongside them. As I've worked with students, I have grown into a dependable, reliable, and committed teacher and teacher leader. I believe my main priority is to serve in the classroom. Because I'm growing and learning alongside them, my students ask at the beginning of each day, "Ms. G., what are we going to learn today?" My experiences as a substitute teacher, long-term substitute, and paraprofessional have instilled in me the importance of relationships, something I am honored to build with my students and their families. As I leave my classroom each day, with papers to grade and emails to answer, I know that the time I spend with my students and fellow teachers is not wasted but will change the future.

What is Genevieve's leadership style? How do you know?

_____

_____

_____

What are Genevieve's core values? How do you know?

_____

_____

_____

What do we know about Genevieve's mindset? What words or phrases teach us about her mindset?

_____

_____

_____

What real-life experiences did Genevieve share that made her unique?

_____

_____

_____

What are the strengths of Genevieve's PLP?

_____

_____

_____

What suggestions would you provide to help Genevieve improve this PLP?

_____

_____

_____

Our Suggestions to Genevieve

We loved Genevieve's obvious passion for her work, which is evident in her writing. However, there were questions remaining that we posed to Genevieve in her revised work (in italics and parentheses below). As you'll see, Genevieve's revised PLP was not a complete overhaul. She was able to keep the main ideas and add more specific details to further illustrate some of the great ideas she already laid out in the first draft.

Leadership is a privilege. *(This is a strong statement, but what does it really mean? Why is it a privilege? Can you provide an example or illustrate instead to hook the reader?)* My daily work with students allows me to get to know them, grow with them, and learn alongside them. *(How? Be specific. Give an example or two.)* As I've worked with students, I have grown into a dependable, reliable, and committed teacher and teacher leader. *(This is probably true, but we need an example. Share an instance when you demonstrated your reliability.)* I believe my main priority is to serve in the classroom. Because I am growing and learning alongside them, my students ask at the beginning of each day, "Ms. G., what are we going to learn today?" *(What are you learning? Maybe think about the content you are teaching. How is it something both you and your students learn from?)* My experiences as a substitute teacher, long-term substitute, and paraprofessional have instilled in me the importance of relationships, something I am honored to build with my students and their families. *(What do you do today to prioritize relationships?)* As I leave my classroom each day, with papers to grade and emails to answer, I know that the time I spend with my students and fellow teachers is not wasted but will change the future. *(How do you want the future to look for you and your students?)*

How would adding specific illustrations and examples change the tone of Genevieve's philosophy?

_____

_____

_____

As an outsider reading this, what do you know about Genevieve without ever meeting her?

_____

_____

_____

What do you wish you knew more about Genevieve? What should she add to make her PLP more personal?

_____

_____

_____

Sample PLP #3

This PLP really showcases the unique perspective of the author. It starts out with a rocky first draft, but once Carl is freed up to speak from the heart, his true philosophy emerges.

Carl's First Draft

I have been a professor of art for 15 years. During this time, I have transitioned into a number of leadership roles on campus, including the assistant chair for the department of art and associate dean for special projects for the college of arts. I have been described as a "quiet" leader, and I work to guide and enable those around me to be the best people they can be. As a leader, my primary core values are accountability, optimism, teamwork, trust, and respect. I believe in collaboration and working with people to accomplish goals.

For me, groups work best when they work together. I believe that good leaders listen twice as much as they talk, and my goal as a leader is to have a positive impact on the people around me without letting obstacles such as conflict interfere with progress. I am an idealist at heart, but I temper my idealism with a healthy dose of reality. For me, it is necessary for the two to coincide, as one cannot work without the other. On the Myers-Briggs scale, I am an INFJ and my five main Gallup Strengths are Achiever, Belief, Connectedness, Learner, and Responsibility. I am a dreamer, but I also possess the understanding to bring my visions to reality. Evidence of my leadership can be seen in a variety of ways, such as in my recruitment efforts for the college of arts and humanities, committee and assessment work on campus, and most notably the public art project that raised $75,000 in scholarships for the university.

As a child, I grew up watching the *Super Friends* cartoon on Saturday mornings. To use a metaphor from the show, faculty and staff are in their own way very much like superheroes, and the university is our "Hall of Justice." I expect faculty and staff to come to work each day and (hopefully) have a positive impact on the students and people around us. However, like superheroes, people have their own strengths and weaknesses. As a leader, I need to understand and leverage my skills and the skills of those I'm leading. Doing so can help move others forward in a positive direction to help students and each other succeed.

What is Carl's leadership style? How do you know?

_____

_____

_____

What are Carl's core values? How do you know?

_____

_____

_____

What do we know about Carl's mindset? What words or phrases teach us about his mindset?

_____

_____

_____

What real-life experiences did Carl share that made him unique?

_____

_____

_____

What are the strengths of Carl's PLP?

_____

_____

_____

What suggestions would you provide to help Carl improve this PLP?

_____

_____

_____

Our Suggestions to Carl

We felt Carl's PLP lacked a personal tone—too many test results, job titles, and explanations. After the first few lines, we were bored and confused as readers. What we loved, however, was his idea to bring in a *Super Friends* connection—a memory from his own childhood—as an outline to illustrate his views of leadership, so we urged him to begin with that and build his PLP around it. Here is how Carl revised his PLP to be more precise, personal, and aligned with his professional demeanor:

I am an experienced art professor and academic leader. During my time in higher education, I have transitioned into a number of leadership roles on campus. Academic leadership, to me, is similar to the cartoon *Super Friends* that I grew up watching as a child. Faculty and staff are very much like superheroes, and the university is like our "Hall of Justice." I appreciate faculty and staff who seek to have a positive impact on the students and people around us. However, like superheroes, people have their own strengths and weaknesses. As a leader, I need to understand and leverage my skills and the skills of those I'm leading. Doing so can help move others, and our organization, forward in a positive direction. I believe in working with people to accomplish goals. I believe that good leaders listen twice as much as they talk. I have been described as a "quiet" leader, and I work to guide and enable those around me to be the best people they can be. Evidence of my leadership can be seen in a variety of ways, including recruitment efforts for the college of arts, committee and assessment work on campus, and, most notably, the public art project that raised $75,000 in scholarships for the university.

How did the tone of Carl's PLP change with his second draft?

_____

_____

_____

What do you wish you knew more about Carl?

_____

_____

_____

What aspects of the PLP make it feel like you know about Carl's experience in education?

_____

_____

_____

Finding Your PLP Voice

As you can see from the examples shared in this chapter, no two PLPs are alike. Just as every leader's journey is unique, so, too, is every philosophy. Embrace your uniqueness. Use the writing process as a series of stages: get it on paper, then set it aside for a while. Then revisit it. Change words, move them around, try new words. As you reflect, rewrite, and redraft your PLP, you will find that time allows ideas to settle and your voice to emerge. As you've seen in the revised PLPs, it's the personal aspects and specific examples that make them engaging to readers. Don't worry about what other philosophies look or sound like, and don't worry what a reader might think of you after the fact. Just do your best to be you on the page.

_____

_____

_____

_____

_____

_____

Your Second, Third, and Fourth Drafts

If you struggle with this process and can't quite get to a cohesive first draft, consider taking a break of a few hours to a few days. By allowing some space between you and your work, you can give your mind a break to reset thoughts, ideas, and logic. Taking a break from your writing can help you view your PLP from a new angle or bring new ideas to the table. It can also provide an opportunity for you to purposefully connect with your history and leadership role.

Sometimes, as we write our PLP, we get overly concerned with what someone will think of us as they read it or whether we are making sense on paper. By setting the piece aside, you create a distance that allows you to then return to it with renewed clarity. In fact, we don't think taking time off from writing is an optional part of the process. In our workshops, we've noticed that those who are most successful with their PLPs are willing to take the time to digest the information, think about how it feels to read the words, and connect with how it depicts a leader's perspective.

Your next step is to begin your second draft. Rearrange and rewrite. Try new words. Explore a new order. Once you feel like your draft is in good shape, share it with a trusted coworker, family member, or friend and ask for constructive feedback. (Later, you will solicit feedback from a more diverse audience.) Ask your initial reader to assess whether your draft provides a true description of your leadership style, lived experiences, mindset, and core values. "Critical friends" like this can provide feedback on leadership qualities not apparent to those outside your school, push you to reflect on leadership attributes, ask questions, probe for justification, and help identify examples of evidence to support your leadership philosophy (Katz, Dack, & Malloy, 2018).

Once you feel comfortable with your draft, move on to the next one, and then the next one after that. We recommend at least four drafts to get to a comprehensive, approachable piece. Use your time reflecting on your work to analyze and further develop your PLP into a more cohesive expression describing your leadership philosophy. Only at the very end should you edit your PLP for typos, grammatical errors, formatting errors, or missing words.

_____

_____

_____

_____

_____

_____

_____

_____

_____

_____

_____

_____

_____

_____

Your Final Draft

Once you have completed several drafts of your PLP and have taken the necessary breaks in between each draft, start composing your final version. The final draft will need revising until it reads smoothly and captures the essence of your leadership philosophy. You've already worked through several drafts, so it is likely that you've purposefully chosen the appropriate words that reflect what you are trying to say. Take time to let your words rest and spend some time reflecting on what you've written.

_____

_____

_____

_____

_____

_____

_____

_____

_____

_____

_____

_____

Conclusion

As you complete your PLP, remember that it expresses who you are, where you have been in your leadership journey, and how you plan to lead moving forward. Sharing this information with those you lead can help keep you motivated and committed to constant improvement. Additionally, your PLP can provide direction and comfort during tough times. It is also important to recognize that every great leader experiences both success and challenges, and that these can be used to fuel the continuous improvement of your PLP (Hegarty, 2015). Remember that failure, with a growth mindset, can lead to innovation and change.

Consider how the day-to-day events in your professional and personal life are affecting your philosophy. Your PLP should be a living document, updated as your real-life experiences change (Yeom, Miller & Delp, 2018).

Reflection Questions

1. Does my PLP really represent who I am in real life?
2. What do I hope people learn about me from my philosophy?
3. How can I inspire others through my philosophy?
4. What do I want to change about myself (e.g., my decision making, leadership, or values), and how do I get started?
5. Am I more than my title? What assumptions do I still need to challenge?
6. How will I use my PLP to guide my day-to-day leadership activities?
7. How will I make updating my PLP part of my ongoing leadership development? How often will I do this?
8. How can I use my PLP to set goals that have clear, definable results?
9. How will I share my completed PLP with those I lead?
10. Where will I post my PLP so I can see it often?

9

Putting My PLP into Practice

Paul spent time at his summer leadership retreat drafting, writing, and revising his PLP. What he had written, he felt, was an accurate reflection of his commitment to students, his love of learning, and how he grew through the ranks from substitute teacher to associate vice principal. Paul posted his PLP to his school website and was surprised when the parent of a student wrote him a personal thank-you email for sharing such a heartfelt piece in his profile. This struck Paul, since he had not really contemplated the extent of the reach of his profile. He knew his PLP was accurate and that teachers and other school leaders would get where he was coming from, but he never considered how parents, students, or school board members might perceive his words. He wondered if he had been professional enough. Had he appropriately addressed readers outside the school? What about that misspelled word in the third sentence—did that ruin his credibility? Paul began to wonder how his PLP would influence perceptions of him. He also wondered when and

how he should revisit the document. Would it ever change? How would
he know when to change it?

You did it! You crafted a working copy of your PLP that reflects your leadership style, core values, mindset, and real-life experiences. Congratulations! Many leaders have not made it this far, but you invested, reflected, and worked hard to get here. So now what do you do? Why go through all this effort only to file the PLP away? Remember that this is meant to be an evolving document—one that changes as you gain more experience, move into different roles, and even change locations or schools.

In this chapter, we show how to put the PLP into action by sharing it with others, soliciting feedback, revising your philosophy, and addressing criticism.

Reflecting on Your Purpose and Audience

It is vitally important for you to consider the purpose and audience for your PLP prior to sharing it. The main purpose of your PLP is probably to tell the story of your leadership journey, explain what you value, and assert who you hope to become. But why is it important for your school community to know these things? How does that change how you lead? How will it change your relationships? Your audience might also include random people on the internet. As such, it's important to consider how your statements, word choice, and overall tone might come off to people who don't know you.

Having a clear purpose and audience also means opening yourself up to criticism and unsolicited feedback. This can be exceptionally difficult when some of your harshest critics include other educators. That being said, if your PLP is authentic, written from what you know to be true and reflective of who you really are, then the audience should not intimidate you—rather, it should inspire you!

Think about what would happen if every member of your leadership team wrote and shared a PLP. How would that change how you view one another? What could you learn from one another? How might it strengthen your school community?

Seeking Feedback

The first step after completing your PLP is to share it. We recommend sharing it with a close colleague or someone with whom you work every day at school, but you should also share it with some others who can help you refine and fine-tune the document. Here are some ideas:

- **Your spouse/partner/best friend:** Sharing your PLP with someone close to you, such as a spouse, partner, or best friend, allows you to feel safe in the sharing process while also gaining insight from someone who has personal knowledge of you as a whole person, not just as a school leader.

- **A teacher in your school:** Sharing with a teacher invites feedback from someone who actively engages with you in your "title." For the most part, teachers observe you during decision making, hear the chatter in the teacher's lounge, and interact with you one-on-one personally and professionally. A teacher will also understand the unique circumstances in your school community (e.g., the makeup of the students, the demands of the parents, the lack or presence of resources).

- **A student:** Students are the heartbeat of our schools. Whether you serve as a principal, instructional leader, coach, or teacher leader, it is imperative that students recognize why you lead the way you do. Granted, they may not bring the life experience or insights from professional settings in the same way as a colleague, but their perceptions and feelings about your leadership are valid and need to be considered.

- **A school leader from a different school:** Educators who serve in leadership positions know the challenges and opportunities of your position. Gathering feedback from someone in a different school setting can help illuminate problematic areas such as bias, unintended language, or unanticipated perceptions.

- **A supervisor:** Sharing your PLP with your supervisor allows for a different type of conversation than usual to take place: one that focuses on your individuality rather than your performance.

- **Parents:** As much as our service is targeted to students and teachers, parents and caretakers are also an integral part of the school community, so it's smart to solicit their feedback. They may not understand the intricacies of your job, but they are the most likely to perceive you as your title and make assumptions about you and your role.

- **A noneducator:** Noneducators can provide feedback to help with clarity, language, and the overall tone of your PLP. They are most likely to point out your use of jargon, unrealistic ambitions, or language that might be exclusionary. Find people you know who are not in the education field at all and see if what you wrote in your PLP makes sense to them.

Consider This

Cooper's job as an instructional coach meant she worked with multiple teachers throughout the year to help strengthen their classroom teaching strategies. She was experienced in providing feedback, working through

difficult conversations, and noticing small details that could improve
student learning. Cooper's PLC team decided to write their PLPs as part
of a yearlong process. As each member of the team drafted and revised,
Cooper began to struggle with the feedback she received from the teachers
she was used to coaching. One was critical of her writing; another
questioned the authenticity of her core values. Cooper wondered if their
criticism was based on her role as an instructional coach whose job was
to help improve the teacher.

1. *What would you tell Cooper about these dynamics?*

_____

_____

_____

_____

2. *What is Cooper's best response to her PLC team members?*

_____

_____

_____

_____

3. *How can Cooper better receive critical feedback?*

_____

_____

_____

_____

Identifying the right people to provide feedback is critical to gaining honest insights into your work. A PLC such as Cooper's is a great place to write PLPs as a team, but it requires a mindset that removes formal titles and accepts feedback in a way that does not cause personal damage to working relationships.

What to Ask When Gathering Feedback

Here are some questions you can ask to ensure the feedback you receive is as helpful as possible:

1. When you read my PLP, what did you learn about me?
2. What do you think I value in my role as a school leader?
3. In what ways do I share my goals or aspirations?
4. What feelings does my PLP lead you to have?
5. What parts of my PLP were confusing or incomplete?
6. What suggestions do you have to make my PLP stronger?
7. What three words would you use to describe me after reading my PLP?
8. Where do you think I should share my PLP?
9. How do you think my PLP will be perceived by others?
10. Do you think my PLP is useful?

When you ask for feedback, first explain what you wrote and why, and then provide a list of questions you want that specific reader to address. We recommend limiting your request to three or four questions so the reader can provide a thoughtful response.

Accepting Feedback

Accepting feedback can be challenging, even for the most resilient among us. It is important to remember that the feedback you receive is not personal criticism—it is insight to help strengthen your work. Listen carefully. Consider the feedback and determine what to do with it. The important piece here is that you are open-minded.

Consider This

Teacher leader Adam invited his principal Jerome to provide some feedback on the PLP he had written over the holiday break. In his feedback, Jerome suggested that Adam revise a few sentences so his core values would be easier to relate to and that he include his professional goals for the future (specifically, the titles of jobs he hoped to hold). Adam was uncomfortable with this; after all, his PLP was designed to share his leadership philosophy, not his professional aspirations. He began to have doubts. Could he be an effective school leader if he did not aspire to be a superintendent? Was being a teacher leader not enough? Did his philosophy need to push him in the direction of a bigger and better title?

1. *What advice would you give Adam about the feedback from Jerome?*

    _____

    _____

    _____

2. *What do you think? Should a PLP include professional aspirations in addition to leadership style, core values, mindset, and real-life experiences? Why or why not?*

    _____

    _____

    _____

3. *If Adam rejects the advice, how should he explain his rationale to Jerome?*

    _____

    _____

    _____

Asking for feedback and accepting feedback are two different processes, and one is a lot easier to do than the other. Welcome this challenge. The purpose of sharing your PLP with specific people and types of readers is to strengthen your work—not to tear you down. Therefore, go into the review process with an open mind and a willingness to hear both criticism and praise.

As writers, we have had our fair share of feedback from readers, editors, and colleagues, and there are a few tips we would like to share with you about the responses you will get when you venture out to share your PLP:

- Positive feedback is just as important as critical feedback, but sometimes we only hear the bad parts. Ask for and listen specifically for what the readers like and appreciate about your writing.
- Critical feedback is necessary for growth. It is not personal and does not make you less of a school leader. It is an opportunity to learn someone else's perception and to consider how your writing might be read in a way you may not have intended.
- Although critical feedback is necessary, you don't always have to make the changes someone suggests. Listen, digest, and consider the feedback (both good and bad), and only then decide whether your writing needs revision.
- Be aware of positive feedback that is really intended to make you feel better but does not address the PLP.
- Avoid the temptation to have someone rewrite your work for you. Let's face it, educators are pretty experienced at feedback and evaluation, but your PLP is yours and yours alone. If someone tries to rewrite your work, consider the suggestion and determine how it best fits with your writing goals.
- Make sure your writing is feedback-ready. That is, do not waste your time or your reader's time by sharing multiple drafts. This is why we have you do some of your drafting within the pages of this book—so you have a safe place to try out new words, rearrange sentences, and eliminate hiccups in your writing.

- Alternate reviewers, since the more times the same person reviews your work, the less likely that person is to see errors, point out unclear concepts, or seek clarification.

You are the author of your PLP. Remember this. You wrote the PLP after investing your time and energy in a rigorous process of self-evaluation and reflection. Feedback is great, but in the end, it is *your* PLP. When you share or post your PLP, you want to feel proud of your work and know that it reflects the fact that you are more than your title. The review process is integral in making sure your writing is clear and that your message is delivered as intended, but in the end, your PLP should be what you want it to be.

Reflecting on Feedback

Once you start the feedback process, it is possible that you may feel overwhelmed or confused by the advice, ideas, or suggestions provided by your readers. This is one reason we suggest you be very specific about who you invite to read and the feedback you seek. What you will find is that each reader will have a different response. Take time to engage in a purposeful reflective practice before conducting any revisions. The following five questions are designed to help you focus on what your reader shares and what you can choose (or choose not) to implement as a result. Think about these questions as you read your reader feedback:

1. What surprised you in the feedback? Why?
2. What did the reader identify as a strength in your PLP? Do you agree? Why or why not?
3. What weaknesses or areas of improvement did the reader suggest? Do you agree with that advice? Why or why not?
4. If you were to change your PLP based on the reader's suggestions, would that change the tone, voice, or feel of your PLP? How so?
5. How do you feel after receiving this feedback?

Publishing Your PLP

The careful writing and revision of your PLP must end at some point, so set a due date. When that due date arrives, you are ready to publish your PLP. This means sharing it with a wider audience than those chosen few from whom you have solicited feedback. It involves two facets: visibility and accessibility. *Visibility* means your PLP can be seen. Parents, teachers, students, and community members can see, read, and understand it. *Accessibility* means your PLP is understandable to a variety of audiences. It is not heavy with jargon or academic language, filled with examples only you understand, or written in such a way that a community member has difficulty comprehending.

By maintaining visibility and accessibility, you invite readers to engage with this very personal process. Taking this step can provoke a feeling of vulnerability but also provide a sense of transparency. What you share with the world should be something you are proud of, something you really feel is a part of your being and a glimpse into who you are beyond your title.

Where to Publish Your PLP

You should wholeheartedly embrace the opportunity to publish your PLP. After all, this might be the first time your school community will think of you as something more than your title. Here are some different places and ways to share your PLP:

- Post your PLP on your school website profile page.
- Share your PLP in your back-to-school letters or in communications sent out by the school.
- Include some or all of your PLP in your email signature.
- Post your PLP on your LinkedIn or Twitter profile.
- Add your PLP to your professional portfolio.
- Develop and share your PLP in PLC or leadership team meetings.

- Print and post your PLP near your work area as a visible reminder to you and those who visit you.
- Share your PLP in new teacher leader meetings as a way to help others understand how you lead and what to expect from you.
- Write your PLP out in the front of your planner or notebook as a reminder to yourself.
- Keep a copy of your PLP in the visor of your car.
- Give a copy of your PLP to a colleague and ask him or her to remind you to revisit it occasionally throughout the year.

Sharing your PLP should be an exciting opportunity for you. In a sense, it should allow you to breathe a little easier knowing that your story is told and that you are more than the role you assume in a school. It can help others get to know you more efficiently and in ways that are in tune with your interests and experiences. In addition, it can help others feel less intimidated or detached—personalizing what used to be a distant relationship due to status or perception.

When and How to Revisit Your PLP

Here are some specific times when it's a good idea to revisit your PLP:

- When you assume a new leadership role or new duties.
- When you change schools or districts.
- When burnout brews, you question your future in education, and you start to wonder why you stay.
- When you apply for a new position or promotion or shift into a different role.
- When things are going especially well, your students are excelling, and you have a natural high when you go home for the day.
- In the middle of summer, when things settle down and you have had some time away from the daily grind of work.
- Upon hiring new staff members.

As you can see, the process of revisiting your philosophy is fluid and open. By reviewing your PLP often and under different circumstances, you revisit your style, core values, mindset, and real-life experiences and you can examine what the PLP means in terms of real life rather than as words on the page.

Maintaining an Annual Revision Schedule

Although you should *revisit* your PLP frequently, *revising* is a different matter. Because you have invested time and energy into the drafting process, solicited reviews from others, and revised your work before publication, you should let the work stand unaltered for a while. See how it compares with your real, lived life. Measure yourself next to the values you attest to in it. We recommend revising your PLP no more or less than once a year to ensure it remains relevant and timely.

Consider This

Robin prepared her PLP through a series of drafts and revisions. She shared it with colleagues and received positive feedback on it. When she posted it on her school profile page at the beginning of her first principalship in a new school, she received an email from a teacher who wondered why Robin felt it was necessary to share her philosophy as part of the school web-site. After all, as the principal, she had a role and duties to perform. The teachers, it seemed, were more concerned about how Robin was going to secure more funding for special-needs students, how she would navigate the out-of-control PTA, and when she was planning to meet with the teachers' union representatives. "You might value honesty and transparency," the teacher wrote, "but here, we value someone who can make decisions that make our lives easier."

1. Robin's enthusiasm to share her PLP was quickly squashed by the teacher's email. What should Robin reflect on before she responds to the teacher?

    _____

    _____

    _____

2. Why is Robin's PLP valuable in light of the situation she faces in her new setting?

    _____

    _____

    _____

3. Craft a message that Robin could send to the teacher that both defends the PLP and acknowledges the teacher's concerns.

    _____

    _____

    _____

Conclusion

The PLP was designed to help us with that inevitable conflict of identities—the clash we feel when we are misunderstood or expected to behave a certain way simply because of our role as a school leader.

Imagine you kept your PLP to yourself. You invested in this book, participated in the assessments, and drafted your PLP. You may have even invited a few friends and colleagues to read your work. Then, as soon as you were done, you pushed the PLP away on your bookshelf. You rarely revisited it. It faded in your memory. Doing this would reinforce the idea that you are OK with people treating you a certain way just because of your title or position. You accept a distance between students or parents who may not understand the real-life experiences that could actually make you more relatable. Your core values are ignored and not prioritized over any other aspect of your life.

By sharing your PLP with your school community, colleagues, and beyond, you are sharing part of your own leadership story. You acknowledge that everyone's story is different and you have unique traits that make you the leader you are today. Publishing is not a means to seek false affirmation or to make a political statement; rather, it is meant to humanize a somewhat impersonal process. It is a method of offering up part of your life story as a way of building relationships and fostering new beginnings.

Reflection Questions

1. How is your newly crafted PLP different than your teaching philosophy?
2. What did you learn from the PLP drafting process?
3. Where do you think you should post/print/share your PLP?
4. How does your PLP demonstrate your unique talents and traits?
5. How does your PLP articulate that you are more than your title to your school community?
6. After you have shared your PLP with an invited reader, how did you feel? What surprised you about the process?
7. Who do you think would most benefit from reading your PLP? How can you best reach that audience?
8. Where can you post your PLP so it is a reminder for you about your philosophy?
9. What concerns you about your PLP?
10. What did you learn about yourself during this process?

10

Our Leadership Philosophies

Words mean more than what is set down on paper. It takes the human voice to infuse them with deeper meaning.

—Maya Angelou

In our time spent with school leaders over the past five years, developing and working through the PLP process, one of the most common inquiries we get is "Can we read *your* PLP?" Of course, we have gone through the process ourselves and found the amount of introspection and reflection to be daunting. What we include here are our original drafts that we wrote months ago and then set aside. We revisited them occasionally, and now that we are writing for you, the reader, as our audience, we prepared our final drafts for this book. This is hard work. The process of drafting, revising, and re-revising our work took several months—and continues today.

What follows are our first and most recent drafts of our own leadership philosophies, along with some thoughts about the process. We hope you find these helpful in your own writing journey.

Gretchen's Leadership Philosophy

Gretchen's First Draft

Two decades working in education—first as a high school teacher, now as a college professor—leave me continuously challenged and inspired to learn more and dive deeper into things I have never considered. I spend a great deal of my spare time wondering, "What if...?" and "I wonder when...?"

My life has been centered around school—from my time as an ambitious young public school student, then as a college student, later as a law student, and then finally as a college professor. Education has been a path to opportunity and unanticipated doors. The walls of schools are what shaped my world view. I anticipate that life and its various adventures will be messy, like a painting swirled by the fingers of a child. I hold firmly to the belief that no one can take education from you—something passed down from my grandmother to my working-class parents and then to me. It is with that mindset that I hang fiercely to my responsibility and commitment to learn from the unique experiences and stories of the people I learn beside in the classroom where I teach. To me, their story is my teacher.

Gretchen's Most Recent Draft

My life has been centered around school—from my time as an ambitious young public school student, then as a college student, later as a law student, and then finally as a college professor. Education has been a path to opportunity and unanticipated doors. The walls of schools are what shaped my world view. Two decades working in education—first as a high school teacher, now as a college professor—leave me continuously challenged and inspired to learn more and dive deeper into things I have never considered. I spend a great deal of my spare time wondering, "What if . . .?" and "I wonder when . . .?"

I am an achiever—I've spent my life reading, writing, and studying in a way to understand what motivates, drives, and inspires people to live authentically. In my work with students, I am known to push for excellence, even if that means making mistakes along the journey of learning. But in my path seeking achievement, I've recognized the value of hard work, sacrifice, and commitment. To me, achievement means nothing if you arrive at your destination isolated and alone. The ability to connect with others makes the journey worthwhile. I embrace this as a means of understanding the imperfections, uniqueness, and value of the individual.

I anticipate that life and its various adventures will be messy, like a painting swirled by the fingers of a child. I hold firmly to the belief that no one can take education from you—something passed down from my grandmother to my working-class parents and then to me. It is with that mindset that I hang fiercely to my responsibility and commitment to learn from the unique experiences and stories of the people I learn beside in the classroom where I teach. To me, their story is my teacher.

Reflection

I learned from this process that being a leader is so individual. Even though we try to categorize people into certain leadership types, groups, or styles, in the end, every person is a unique mix of qualities. I learned that my leadership philosophy should tell my story—not who I hope to be someday or how I hope other people perceive me to be.

The challenge for me was in figuring out how my mindset guides my professional decisions. I tend to like stability and predictability, which can really lean toward a fixed mindset, yet I also want to learn to be more willing to try and fail—something that indicates a growth mindset. Therefore, the process taught me more about this fascinating aspect of leadership and how that can be the crux for many of our decisions.

Taking the assessment results and then making them make sense in my professional life was the most difficult aspect of the process for me. It would be easiest to just come out and say I am a guiding leader who values responsibility, trust, and accountability, but that really doesn't capture who I am—so I had to use those as building blocks to demonstrate to the reader how I put these things into practice in real-life situations.

I love that my leadership is based on my journey in education. That isn't true for everyone, and I certainly have experiences outside of education (I am a lawyer, mom, author, and real person), yet my professional life has always been focused on education. Therefore, to me, that common theme allowed me to continue to center what I was working toward in understanding and sharing my leadership philosophy.

I've shared my personal leadership philosophy at workshops, on my social media, and in marketing interviews I've done to help recruit students to the program in which I teach. I happen to teach leadership students in graduate school, so the ability to quickly identify my leadership philosophy gives students some reassurance that I've seriously thought about leadership and am centered on who I am as a leader.

The reflective steps in this process had the greatest influence on me. I'm an assessment junkie, so I love taking tests to figure out what personality style I have, what leadership traits I practice, and even just mindless things like what sort of cocktail I would be, given my personality. I love the challenge of looking at a list and being forced to choose an answer. It's so different than the writing process where the page always starts blank. Being forced to make some decisions compelled me to put a name on what I do. I revisit this as I face difficult choices or professional opportunities. I go back to "How does this fit my core values?" and "What type of mindset does this make me engage with?" If nothing else, the PLP process has taught me that leadership is something that anyone can do—it's just a matter of telling your story in an authentic way and utilizing the attributes and assets you've gained throughout your life's journey to somehow help others forge their own paths.

Vicki's Leadership Philosophy

Vicki's First Draft

Henry Ford said, "If everyone is moving forward together, then success takes care of itself." Through my professional experiences, from serving pancakes to teaching in higher education and everything in between, I have learned that connectivity, collaboration, and communication—**the three *C*s**—are the keys to successfully moving forward as a team, department, or organization.

When the environment, whether a restaurant or an academic department, is focused on sharing ideas and insights to achieve a common goal, team members tend to feel **connected** to something bigger than themselves. This breaks down silos and creates a workplace where employees feel valued.

A **collaborative** workplace is established from the top down—whether it be a team lead or assistant program director. To create this culture, I maintain an open-door policy that encourages idea sharing, debate, and discussion to build trusting relationships. To facilitate interactions and develop strong relationships between employees, I invest in development opportunities and social events.

Though it's sometimes challenging, I provide honest and transparent **communication**, providing both the positive and negative aspects of a situation to facilitate decision making and advance nimbleness to react to the market demand. In all that I do, I know that those I work with and for are the center of what I do and aspire to achieve.

Vicki's Most Recent Draft

Henry Ford said, "If everyone is moving forward together, then success takes care of itself." Through my professional experiences, from serving pancakes to teaching in higher education and everything in between, I have learned that connectivity, collaboration, and communication—**the three *C*s**—are the keys to successfully moving forward as a team, department, or organization.

When the environment, whether a restaurant or an academic department, is focused on sharing ideas and insights to achieve a common goal, team members tend to feel **connected** to something bigger than themselves. I know that I am more invested in my work when I am passionate about it. In order for me to do this, I focus on building strong personal and professional relationships with my colleagues, inspiring trust and transparency, and hopefully building bonds that last beyond the walls of the organization.

A **collaborative** workplace is established by the leader. To create this culture, I maintain an open-door policy that encourages idea sharing, debate, and discussion to build trusting relationships. To facilitate interactions and develop strong relationships between employees, I invest in development opportunities and social events.

Though it's sometimes challenging, I provide honest and transparent **communication**, providing both the positive and negative aspects of a situation to facilitate decision making. I've witnessed effective and ineffective messaging, and I understand the impact it has on a person and organization. My work history spans from service jobs to nonprofit roles to leading in higher education. In all of these roles, I have appreciated the opportunity to make informed decisions and to be inclusive in that process.

In all that I do, I know that those I work with and for are the center of why I do what I do. My focus on people—and their stories—is really what drives my leadership. I strive to be present, attentive, and willing to adapt. While I strive to do well, I know that I cannot achieve alone, so relationships are the foundation of what I do.

Reflection

Writing a PLP is not a quick process! It took me multiple drafts and feedback from my trusted circle of colleagues to create a statement that I was proud to share with the world. I had lots of ideas, themes, angles, and stories I considered for my PLP. Having ideas was not the challenging part—narrowing them down and deciding how I wanted to represent myself was. Additionally, I had lots of thoughts swirling around in my head when I started the writing process, which made me anxious that I might forget something. Once I got my thoughts down on paper, I wasn't as anxious because I knew my ideas were documented and I could go back to them as needed.

The beginning of the statement was the hardest for me to write because I consider the first few sentences of any written work the most critical. You either hook the reader or you don't, and I wanted to hook the reader! I wanted to start my PLP in a way that was authentic to who I am—considering my leadership style, lived experiences, mindset, core values—and who I am on a personal level. I love quotes; I have a quote journal, a Pinterest board full of quotes, and sticky notes full of quotes on my office wall. Therefore, starting my PLP with a quote seemed like a natural fit.

I also love that my PLP has ideas, thoughts, and examples from all my professional experiences. As I created my PLP, I had my résumé handy to reflect on what I learned from each position.

I shared my PLP with students in the capstone course I teach. They are working toward becoming health and wellness coaches. Part of my role as a college instructor is to be able to facilitate conversations about what direction they want to pursue in that industry. The PLP opens the door to that discussion—it shows my students how I work and where I've been and gives them a glimpse into who I am as a person. I have also used the PLP in my professional profile online so anyone who visits my page can get a quick sense about me without having to read my entire résumé.

By using my résumé to guide the PLP writing process, I've been able to represent every professional experience I've had in some word, phrase, or example, giving more context to who I am as a leader. My outlook didn't really change by going through the PLP process, but the process did solidify that everyone is a leader in some capacity in every role and that all our experiences help shape us into who we are.

Final Note from the Authors

This is where our creative process ends. We hope you will return to this book frequently as you move into changing roles and different seasons of life. Writing a PLP is challenging, but it is also such an important step for a reflective, engaged leader. We hope you found this process meaningful and rewarding—and will continue to for many years to come as you revisit your PLP. Stay committed to your leadership journey, and be kind to yourself as you lead others.

References

Amanchukwu, R., Stanley, G., & Ololube, N. (2015). A review of leadership theories, principles and styles and their relevance to educational management. *Management, (5)*1, 6–15.

Bass, B. M., & Avolio, B. J. (Eds.) (1994). *Improving organizational effectiveness through transformational leadership.* Thousand Oaks, CA: Sage.

Beatty, J. E., Leigh, J. S., & Dean, K. L. (2009). Philosophy rediscovered: Exploring the connections between teaching philosophies, educational philosophies, and philosophy. *Journal of Management Education, 33*(1), 99–114.

Browne, M. (2017). Developing a teaching philosophy. *Journal of Effective Teaching, 17*(3), 59–63.

Calinog, C. (2013). The story of my life: Developing authentic leaders [blog post]. Retrieved from *Northwestern School of Education and Social Policy* at www.sesp .northwestern.edu/masters-learning-and-organizational-change/knowledge-lens /stories/2013/the-story-of-my-life-developing-authentic-leaders.html

Carr, B. (2013, April 11). Live your core values: 10-minute exercise to increase your success [blog post]. Retrieved from *TapRoot* at www.taproot.com/live-your-core -values-exercise-to-increase-your-success

Chism, N. V. N. (1998). Developing a philosophy of teaching statement. *Essays on Teaching Excellence, 9*(3), 1–2.

Coppola, B. P. (2002). Writing a statement of teaching philosophy. *Journal of College Science Teaching, 31*(7), 448–453.

Creighton, J. L. (2019, September 22). Reframing your life story: Changing your story may change your life [blog post]. Retrieved from *Psychology Today* at www.psychologytoday.com/ie/blog/loving-through-your-differences/201909 /reframing-your-life-story?amp

Daft, R. L. (2015). *The leadership experience* (7th ed.). Boston: Cengage Learning.

Doyle, A. (2020). Interview question: "What is your teaching philosophy?" [blog post]. Retrieved from *The Balance Careers* at www.thebalancecareers.com/job-interview -answer-what-is-your-teaching-philosophy-2063859

Dweck, C. S. (2016). *Mindset: The new psychology of success.* Ballantine Books.

Ebrahimji, A. (2020, January 30). This teacher's shoes were stolen from his classroom, so his students surprised him with new ones. Retrieved from *CNN* at www.cnn.com /2020/01/30/us/new-shoes-teacher-trnd/index.html

Einhorn, E. (2020). When coronavirus closed schools, some Detroit students went missing from class. These educators had to find them. Retrieved from *NBC News* at www.nbcnews.com/news/education/when-coronavirus-closed-schools-some -detroit-students-went-missing-class-n1227796

Farrace, B. (2020). Principals say pandemic conditions are accelerating their plans to leave the principalship [blog post]. Retrieved from *National Association of Secondary School Principals* at https://blog.nassp.org/2020/08/21/principals -say-pandemic-conditions-are-accelerating-their-plans-to-leave-the-principalship

Ferlazzo, L. (2018, March 30). Response: Educators share who influenced their teaching. Retrieved from *EdWeek.org* at www.edweek.org/leadership/opinion -response-educators-share-who-influenced-their-teaching/2018/03

Freudenberger, H. J. (1980). *Burnout: The high cost of high achievement.* New York: Doubleday.

Goodyear, G. E., & Allchin, D. (1998). Statements of teaching philosophy. *To Improve the Academy*, 17(1), 103–121.

Grundman, H. G. (2006). Writing a teaching philosophy statement. *Notices of the AMS*, 53, 1329–1333.

Hegarty, N. (2015). The growing importance of teaching philosophy statements and what they mean for the future: Why teaching philosophy statements will affect you. *Journal of Adult Education*, 44(2), 28–30.

Hirschman, C., & Voloshin, I. (2007). The structure of teenage employment: Social background and the jobs held by high school seniors. *Research in Social Stratification and Mobility*, 25(3), 189–203.

Hoerr, T. (September, 2013). Good failures. *Educational Leadership*, 71(1), 84–85.

Katz, S., Dack, L. A., & Malloy, J. (2018). *The intelligent, responsive leader.* Thousand Oaks, CA: Corwin.

Kaufman Hogan, L. (2014). 8 lessons we learned from our first jobs. Retrieved from *pbs.org* at www.pbs.org/newshour/economy/8-lessons-learned-first-jobs

Kearns, K. D., & Sullivan, C. S. (2011). Resources and practices to help graduate students and postdoctoral fellows write statements of teaching philosophy. *Advances in Physiology Education*, 35(2), 136–145.

Khazan, O. (2021, March 21). Only your boss can cure your burnout. Retrieved from *The Atlantic* at www.theatlantic.com/politics/archive/2021/03/how-tell-if-you -have-burnout/618250

Kotter, J. P. (2000). *Leading change.* Boston: Harvard Business Review.

LAMA. (2018). Lessons learned: How your first job can influence your future career [blog post]. Retrieved from *Medium* at https://medium.com/@lama_app_64466 /lessons-learned-how-your-first-job-can-influence-your-future-career-735bcd687ff9

Lassiter, C. (2017). Leading from a courageous mindset. *Instructional Leader, 30.* Retrieved from https://tepsa.org/wp-content/uploads/2018/10/lassitersample.pdf

Lencioni, P. M. (2002). Make your values mean something [blog post]. Retrieved from *Harvard Business Review* at https://hbr.org/2002/07/make-your-values-mean-something

Levin, S., Scott, C., Yang, M., Leung, M., & Bradley, K. (2020). Supporting a strong stable principal workforce: What matters and what can be done [blog post]. Retrieved from *National Association of Secondary School Principals* at www.nassp.org /nassp-and-lpi-research-agenda/nassp-lpi-research-report

Lipman, V. (2017, May 9). Why confidence is always a leader's best friend. Retrieved from *Forbes* at www.forbes.com/sites/victorlipman/2017/05/09/why-confidence-is -always-a-leaders-best-friend/?sh=ffa032147bef

Michel, A. (2016). Burnout and the brain. Retrieved from the *Association for Psychological Science* at www.psychologicalscience.org/observer/burnout-and-the-brain

Mooney, N. J., & Mausbach, A. T. (2008). *Align the design: A blueprint for school improvement.* Alexandria, VA: ASCD.

Nasri, G. (2014, January 15). 6 personal philosophies that shaped successful entrepreneurs [blog post]. Retrieved from *Fast Company* at www.fastcompany.com /3024831/the-personal-philosophies-that-shape-todays-successful-innovators

Northouse, P. G. (2015). *Introduction to leadership: Concepts and practice.* Thousand Oaks, CA: Sage.

Platt, R. (2018). When values and mission guide your decisions [blog post]. Retrieved from *MiddleWeb* at www.middleweb.com/39138/when-values-and-mission-guide -your-decisions

Robert K. Greenleaf Center for Servant Leadership. (2016). What is servant leadership? Retrieved from www.greenleaf.org/what-is-servant-leadership

Sadowsky, J. (2020). The value of processing your life's experiences [blog post]. Retrieved from *JohnSadowsky.com* at www.johnsadowsky.com/value-processing-lifes -experiences

Safir, S. (2019, November). Six ways to support and sustain quality principals [blog post]. Retrieved from *National Association of Secondary School Principals* at www.nassp.org/2019/11/01/principal-well-being-a-missing-link

Salisbury, M. (2019). "Hey, hey, it's Mama J"–New principal leads with P.O.W.E.R. [blog post]. Retrieved from *The Budget Online* at https://lhsbudget.com /archive/2019/10/02/hey-hey-its-mama-j-new-principal-leads-with-p-o-w-e-r

Smith, B. S. (2016). The role of leadership style in creating a great school. Retrieved from *Saskatchewan Education Leadership Unit* at https://selu.usask.ca/documents /research-and-publications/srrj/SRRJ-1-1-Smith.pdf

St. Thomas University. (2018). What is transactional leadership? [webpage]. Retrieved from *STU Online* at https://online.stu.edu/articles/education/what-is-transactional -leadership.aspx#definition

Tribune Media Wire. (2019, January 24). School official quits after charges she pretended sick student was her son to get him treatment [blog post]. Retrieved

from *WREG Memphis* at https://wreg.com/news/superintendent-charged-with
-fraud-for-using-own-insurance-to-help-ill-student

Waters, J. T., Marzano, R. J., & McNulty, B. (2004). Leadership that sparks learning. *Educational Leadership, 61*(7), 48–51.

World Health Organization (2019). Burn-out an "occupational phenomenon": International classification of diseases [blog post]. Retrieved from the *World Health Organization* at www.who.int/news/item/28-05-2019-burn-out-an
-occupational-phenomenon-international-classification-of-diseases

Yeom, Y., Miller, M. A., & Delp, R. (2018). Constructing a teaching philosophy: Aligning beliefs, theories, and practice. *Teaching and Learning in Nursing, 13*(3), 131–134.

Index

About the Authors

Gretchen Oltman is an author, attorney, and educator. She works as an associate professor of interdisciplinary studies at Creighton University, where she leads a program for graduate students pursuing degrees in leadership. Prior to this, she was a high school English teacher. She holds a law degree from the University of Nebraska College of Law, a PhD in educational studies from the University of Nebraska–Lincoln, an MA in teaching from the University of Louisville, and a BA in English from the University of Nebraska–Lincoln. She is licensed to practice law in Nebraska and to work as a teacher and administrator for grades 7–12. She is the author or coauthor of *Violence in Student Writing: A School Administrator's Guide; Law Meets Literature: A Novel Approach to the English Classroom; The Supreme 15: Cases and Study Materials for the AP Government and Politics Exam; The Themes That Bind Us: Simplifying*

U.S. Supreme Court Cases for the Social Studies Classroom; and *Prepare to Chair: Leading the Dissertation and Thesis Process.* She regularly presents for ASCD, the Education Law Association, and the National Council for Teachers of English.

 **Vicki Bautista** is an assistant professor at Creighton University in the department of interdisciplinary studies. She serves as the assistant program director for the MS in integrative health and wellness. She received a BA from the University of Texas–El Paso in health science with a minor in community health and an MA from the University of Nebraska–Omaha in health education. She earned her EdD in interdisciplinary leadership at Creighton University, focusing on department chairs and well-being. Prior to working at Creighton, she was employed in a variety of health promotion settings including nonprofit, government, and research in the high school setting. She presents regularly on the topics of leadership and well-being, self-care, and personal leadership philosophies.

Related ASCD Resources: Leadership

At the time of publication, the following resources were available (ASCD stock numbers in parentheses).

Adventures in Teacher Leadership: Pathways, Strategies, and Inspiration for Every Teacher by Rebecca Mieliwocki and Joseph Fatheree (#118033)

The Artisan Teaching Model for Instructional Leadership: Working Together to Transform Your School by Kenneth Baum and David Krulwich (#116041)

Balanced Leadership for Powerful Learning: Tools for Achieving Success in Your School by Bryan Goodwin, Greg Cameron, and Heather Hein (#112025)

Coherent School Leadership: Forging Clarity from Complexity by Michael Fullan and Lyle Kirtman (#118040)

Committing to the Culture: How Leaders Can Create and Sustain Positive Schools by Steve Gruenert and Todd Whitaker (#119007)

Design Thinking for School Leaders: Five Roles and Mindsets That Ignite Positive Change by Alyssa Gallagher and Kami Thordarson (#118022)

Leadership for Learning: How to Bring Out the Best in Every Teacher, 2nd Edition by Carl Glickman and Rebecca West Burns (#121007)

Leading in Sync: Teacher Leaders and Principals Working Together for Student Learning by Jill Harrison Berg (#118021)

The Learning Leader: How to Focus School Improvement for Better Results, 2nd Edition by Douglas B. Reeves (#118003)

Other Duties as Assigned: Tips, Tools, and Techniques for Expert Teacher Leadership by Jan Burgess and Donna Bates (#109075)

The Principal 50: Critical Leadership Questions for Inspiring Schoolwide Excellence by Baruti K. Kafele (#115050)

Teacher Leadership That Strengthens Professional Practice by Charlotte Danielson (#105048)

For up-to-date information about ASCD resources, go to www.ascd.org. You can search the complete archives of *Educational Leadership* at www.ascd.org/el.

ASCD myTeachSource®

Download resources from a professional learning platform with hundreds of research-based best practices and tools for your classroom at http://myteach-source.ascd.org/

For more information, send an email to member@ascd.org; call 1-800-933-2723 or 703-578-9600; send a fax to 703-575-5400; or write to Information Services, ASCD, 1703 N. Beauregard St., Alexandria, VA 22311–1714 USA.

THE WHOLE CHILD

The ASCD Whole Child approach is an effort to transition from a focus on narrowly defined academic achievement to one that promotes the long-term development and success of all children. Through this approach, ASCD supports educators, families, community members, and policymakers as they move from a vision about educating the whole child to sustainable, collaborative actions.

What's Your Leadership Story? relates to the **supported** tenet. *For more about the ASCD Whole Child approach, visit* **www.ascd.org/wholechild.**

WHOLE CHILD
TENETS

1 HEALTHY
Each student enters school healthy and learns about and practices a healthy lifestyle.

2 SAFE
Each student learns in an environment that is physically and emotionally safe for students and adults.

3 ENGAGED
Each student is actively engaged in learning and is connected to the school and broader community.

4 SUPPORTED
Each student has access to personalized learning and is supported by qualified, caring adults.

5 CHALLENGED
Each student is challenged academically and prepared for success in college or further study and for employment and participation in a global environment.